WADSWORTH PHILOSOPHERS SERIES

ON

RUSSELL

S. Jack Odell
The University of Maryland

Wadsworth
Thomson Learning

Australia • Canada • Denmark • Japan • Mexico • New Zealand • Philippines
Puerto Rico • Singapore • Spain • United Kingdom • United States

COPYRIGHT © 2000 Wadsworth, a division of Thomson Learning.
Thomson Learning is a trademark used herein under license.

ALL RIGHTS RESERVED. No part of this work covered by the copyright
hereon may be reproduced or used in any form or by any means—graphic,
electronic, or mechanical, including photocopying, recording, taping, Web
distribution, or information storage and retrieval systems—without the
written permission of the publisher.

Printed in the United States of America
1 2 3 4 5 6 7 03 02 01 00 99

For permission to use material from this text, contact us:
Web: www.thomsonrights.com
Fax: 1-800-730-2215
Phone: 1-800-730-2214

For more information, contact:
Wadsworth/Thomson Learning
10 Davis Drive
Belmont, CA 94002-3098
USA
.www.wadsworth.com

ISBN: 0-534-57616-8

Contents

Introduction

Unlike many important twentieth century philosophers, Russell is a philosopher in the traditional sense of the word. Like Aristotle, he addressed all the standard issues of philosophy. His most influential contributions were in logic, the foundations of mathematics, and the theory of meaning, but he also wrote extensively on the theory of knowledge. In addition, he wrote on ethics, the meaning of life, metaphysics, political and social philosophy, and the nature and relevance of philosophy. He also made contribution to topics which have been subsumed under the heading of the philosophy of science, as well as to topics which are now staked out by those philosophers who classify themselves as cognitive scientists.

I will discuss Russell's views concerning all of these topics. I will also discuss his relationships with important historical philosophers (Plato, Descartes, and Hume) and certain twentieth century ones as well (Wittgenstein, Moore, Austin, Strawson, and Quine,) especially where the views of these latter philosophers collide with those of Russell.

Certain themes permeate Russell's work, and they are intertwined with one another. For example, Russell is a thoroughly committed reductionist. Perhaps his major accomplishment is the development, if not origination, of the analytic method in philosophy. At the core of this method lies the assumption that the only way to get to the truth about the nature of things is to reduce by analysis the macro-appearances of things to their micro-realities. It is an assumption shared with and inspired by both chemistry and

Cartesianism. None can doubt that the incredible success of modern chemistry is the result of the explicit adoption of this assumption. Descartes' method of doubt consists in starting with those aspects of human existence which appear to be grounded in experience and indubitable, and subjecting them to critical scrutiny, labeling as uncertain anything which can be doubted. The underlying assumption of both chemistry and Cartesianism being that things are far from being as they appear to be. The combined outcome of both efforts is to reveal that our understanding of the physical objects of the world, such as tables, chairs, trees, cats, rats, bats, etc., is, at best, illusory and misleading.

Russell believed that mathematics could be reduced to or derived from logic. He also believed that all natural languages could, in spite of their apparent differences in structure, be demonstrated to be grounded in a universal logic. And since he also believed that logic's structure could be demonstrated to correspond to the structure of the world, he was convinced that logic was the essential tool of philosophy. With Alfred North Whitehead, Russell attempted to show that mathematics could indeed be reduced to or derived from logic, and with Wittgenstein he attempted to establish that natural languages are grounded in a universal logic, and that reality is mirrored in this logic.

Although convinced that he and Whitehead, and he and Wittgenstein, had succeeded in their respective endeavors, he did not consider logic to be synonymous with philosophy. He believed that philosophy contained another important ingredient. That ingredient, according to Russell is mysticism.

In spite of appearances to the contrary, appearances based upon the fact that he was such an avid defender of both science and logic, Russell retained throughout much of his life a keen interest in mysticism, and tried to reconcile it with his dedication to scientific and logical approaches to philosophy. His most notable effort in this direction was *Mysticism and Logic*. In it he claimed that many of "the greatest men who have been philosophers", including Hereclitus and Plato, have felt:

> the need both of science and of mysticism: the attempt to harmonize the two was what made their life, and what must for all its arduous uncertainty, make philosophy, to some minds, a greater thing than either science or religion.[1]

He not only shared and debated this idea with other professional philosophers, but with friends and those he loved. One of his most enduring relationships was with Lady Ottoline Morrell, and its basis was not only mutual physical attraction, but also their shared interest in mysticism.

Because his life was nearly as interesting and unique as his philosophy, I will begin with a vignette of it. Then, because of its great importance to him, and because his contributions to its development were objectively so important, the discussion will turn to and provide a critical exposition of his work on logic and mathematics. In doing so, it will explain how his conception of logic determined his views regarding the nature and importance of philosophy, as well as his metaphysics. For Russell, these subjects are so intimately related that it is nearly impossible to discuss them independently.

Nearly as closely related to his views on logic and mathematics as those on philosophy and reality are his views regarding meaning and language. For this reason, I will explicate them next. I will then discuss his views on the nature and extent of human knowledge. After completing my discussion of his theory of knowledge, I will treat briefly his views on a topic much discussed in cognitive scientist circles---the mind-body problem. Following my discussion of this topic, I will turn to his views regarding ethics. In the last chapter, I will cover his views regarding God, Religion, the meaning of life, and the significance of mysticism.

I will devote the most space to his contributions regarding the foundations of logic and mathematics, the theory of meaning, and metaphysics. I will do so because it is in these areas that Russell was most original and influential. I will, however, spend more time on his ethics than is commonly done. My reason for doing this is that I think Russell's work on ethics is both more original and more defensible than either his critics or his defenders seem to think.

Endnotes

[1] Russell (1927) p. 16

I
The Man

Bertrand Russell, "Bertie," to his friends, was one of the more unique and fascinating human beings the modern world has produced. He was a mathematician, philosopher, educator, political activist, feminist, anti-communist, Lord of the British Empire, recipient of the Order of Merit, a Nobel Laureate, an Honorary Fellow of the British Academy, and a prodigious writer   He lived for nearly a century (b. May 18, 1872 d. February 2, 1970) and he continued to be active within weeks of this death. Although spindly and unathletic in build, he was uncommonly vigorous and physically capable, a fact testified to by his having survived the crash of "flying- boat," which was attempting to land on frigid northern waters, when he was 76 years old. The plane failed to land on the water at the correct angle, killing nineteen passengers. He survived by swimming to safety. He was asked how he felt while he was swimming for his life, and is reputed to have replied, in typical Russellian brevity, "cold."

He was married four times. He sired his last child at age sixty six. The forth time he married he was eighty, and his bride was over thirty years his junior. His youngest son Conrad remembers how agile his father was at ninety-five, often climbing over the rails of the balcony of their home in North Wales to get a better view of the afternoon sun-drenched Snowden Mountains. At eighty-eight, he still attended and spoke at rallies for nuclear disarmament, and engaged in a televised transatlantic exchange with Edward Teller, the so-called "father of the H-bomb." Just two days before he died, he publicly condemned Israel for bombing Egypt, claiming that the Israelis excuse, based on the past sins of the Egyptians, was nothing more than hypocrisy.

Russell's childhood was anything but happy. He was born into the privileged class, but misfortune was to characterize his early years. He lost his mother just after his second birthday, and his father before he turned four. After the death of his father, he was sent to live with his grandparents, Lord and Lady John Russell. His grandfather died just two years later, and as a result, his early education and training was under the direction of his grandmother. She was a stern and religious woman. Life with her at her home, Pembroke Lodge, was oppressive. It was a life filled with what he would later refer to as "foolish prohibitions." The fact that so many things were prohibited at Pembroke caused Russell to become an expert at concealment, and deceit--impulses which he had to struggle against throughout his lifetime. His grandmother provided very little emotional support, which created in Russell an insatiable need for affection and love. He was desperately lonely, and this led him to feel alienated from other persons. Throughout his life he looked for people he hoped would fulfill these needs. His needs were so great, however, that few if anyone ever managed to satiate them. His grandmother's piety, and her insistence that he become as religious as she was, led him to both embrace and rebel against religion. Her religious beliefs were not based upon intellectual grounds. Russell's early religious beliefs reflected those of his grandmother, but his inquisitive and rational impulses, fed by his need to free himself from her unfounded prohibitions, would eventually lead him to reject all forms of organized religion.

Early in his life, due to the efforts of his brother Frank, he was introduced to Euclid's geometry, a subject which greatly excited him, and led him in the direction of mathematics and logic. It was not until he was twenty-eight, however, that this interest led him to the International Congress of Philosophy in Paris in the year 1900. He later described this year as "the most important year in my intellectual life."[1] It was here that Russell met the Italian logician and mathematician, Peano. Peano had already developed a form of symbolic logic, which Russell quickly mastered. Russell then developed a notation of his own based upon Peano's, and extended Peano's logic to the analysis of relations. His work impressed the influential Cambridge mathematician and philosopher Alfred North Whitehead, which led them

5

to collaborate and eventually produce, *Principia Mathematica*.

Principia Mathematica is one of the most widely discussed and influential books ever written on the foundations of Mathematics, a fact which remains true in spite of the devastating critique launched in 1931 by of one of this century's greatest mathematicians, Kurt Godel. Godel was able to prove that the axiomatic system it introduced to generate all number-theoretic truths, and thereby to establish that all of mathematics could be derived from logic, could not, nor could any such axiomatic system, avoid being inconsistent. Nevertheless, the efforts of Russell and Whitehead provided a much refined and illuminated forum and departure point for the discovery and explication of various surprising and immensely significant truths about formal systems.

Russell's early work in philosophy was influenced by his teachers at Cambridge, James Ward, and G. F. Stout, and by the Hegelian or Absolute Idealists, F. H. Bradley, and J. Ellis McTaggart. For a while he became a Hegelian. He was also influenced by his friend and protégé G.E. Moore. Moore, who was at the time he met Russell an aspiring classicist at Cambridge, impressed Russell with his philosophical acumen. Russell eventually persuaded Moore to turn his attention from classics toward philosophy. Subsequently, it was probably Moore who led Russell to abandon the Idealist's approach. In his autobiographical sketch for the *Library of Living Philosophers* volume on his philosophy, Moore describes his first encounter with McTaggart. The encounter took place at a tea in Cambridge which had been arranged by Russell. Moore recollects:

> ...and McTaggart, in the course of conversation had been led to express his well-known view that Time is unreal. This must have seemed to me then (as it still does) a perfectly monstrous proposition, and I did my best to argue against it. I don't suppose I argued at all well; but I think I was persistent and found quit a lot of different things to say in answer to McTaggart. It must have been owing to what I said on such occasions as this that Russell came to think I had some aptitude for philosophy.[2]

With Ludwig Wittgenstein, his sometime pupil and colleague, more the latter than the former, he generated two of the most widely discussed and influential philosophical movements of the first half of the present century: logical atomism and logical positivism. Although it is extremely difficult to find a philosopher today who would confess to being either an atomist or a positivist, Russell's "Papers on Logical Atomism," and Wittgenstein's *Tractatus Logico Philosophicus*, are still widely studied in philosophy departments throughout the world.[3]

He and his second wife Dora, motivated by the absence in England of a school progressive enough to meet their objectives, decided in 1927 to start their own, which they named Beacon Hill School. They discouraged any kind of religious dogmas by refusing to offer any religious training. They treated all religions as simply historical practices to be studied and contrasted with one another, without expressing favoritism for any one religion over another. They allowed the children considerable freedom of expression, allowing them to frolic about, and to exercise in the nude. Although unpopular both with the press and the traditionalists, who dominated education in England at that time, the school was worthy of respect. Russell was was never satisfied with it. He was never able find the Aristotelian mean between allowing the students too much freedom on the one hand, and imposing too much authority on the other.

His political activism led to his arrest and imprisonment on two separate occasions. Toward the end of the World War I, he was incarcerated for his efforts on behalf of pacifism, specifically for casting dispersion upon the United States. He had suggested in an editorial for the *Tribunal* (May 18, 1918) that should the British government not accept the German overtures for peace, the continuation of the hostilities would led to starvation and insurrection throughout Europe. And this state of affairs would, he claimed, lead to the garrisoning of American troops in England and France. In England, Russell insinuated, this force might very well intimidate British strikers just as it had done against strikers in America.

Russell served six months. He spent his confinement engaged in philosophical research. In his eighty-ninth year, he was again sentenced to prison. This time he was convicted for inciting the public to civil disobedience in opposition to nuclear warfare. Because of his advanced age, his two month sentence was reduced to two weeks in the prison hospital.

Throughout his life, Russell was an staunch feminist. In 1906, he joined the National Union of Women's Suffrage (NUWSS), and was elected to its Executive Committee. In 1907, the NUWSS asked him to run for a vacated seat in Parliament under the banner of Woman's Suffrage. He agreed to do so since there was no chance he would actually be elected. It was a forgone conclusion that the seat would go to the Conservative or Tory candidate. He was attacked both by men, and to Russell's surprise, women. He stood his ground, and, surprisingly, received many more votes than any non-Tory could have expected to receive. Throughout the remainder of his life he could always be depended upon to engage in debate on the behalf of women. He detested the idea that men were superior to women. He thought it degrading not only to women, but also to men. His position on many social issues was far ahead of its time. He argued in support of euthanasia, abolition of the death penalty, and sexual freedom at a time when, for most people, such views were unthinkable.

As a writer his output was astounding. He published hundreds of essays on all sorts of topics, from reasons for not being a Christian to war crimes in Vietnam. In his lifetime he produced over three thousand works. He wrote something nearly every day of his life. In addition to being the author of many books and essays on innumerable topics, he was a constant letter writer. Letter writing served him as a means for making and retaining men and woman as friends and confidants. He was better able to express his feelings for others in his letters than he was able to do in person. He was also fond of recording in journal format his various thoughts and feelings. Because of his prodigious letter writing and his personal journal we possess an unparalleled transcript of his inner life. This rich and revealing transcript enables the biographer to determine the answers to almost any question he or she might have regarding Russell's feelings, beliefs, attitudes, motives, and concerns about most subjects. It also provides a detailed record of his interests, various loves, friendships, failures, and sins.

Russell also had literary aspirations. From time to time during his life he indulged himself by fantasizing that he was a Bohemian novelist, living in a garret with whomever happened to be the woman of the moment. He did, in 1912, collaborate with Ottoline Morrell on the conception, but not on the execution, of a novel, *The Perplexities of John Forstice*. The central character, Forstice, a Faustian sort of character, is a fictionalized version of Russell's idea of himself. Throughout the novel, Forstice engages in debate with various other characters who personify a wide range of perspectives on the "true" nature of human existence, all of which most probably represent various stages in Russell's own intellectual development. Unhappily, no one with any appreciation for the talents required of great fiction writers was impressed with this novel. Great fiction writers are able to dramatize the everyday events of our lives, and to look deeply into the inner lives of their subjects, their motives, fears, hatreds, misgivings, etc., and by so doing cause us to see things in unique and different ways. Russell's novel is entirely devoid of dramatic force, and its characters are stilted and wooden. It can only be appreciated if one thinks of it as an unusual and uncommon forum for philosophical debate -- an academic exercise.

Russell often expressed feelings of estrangement from others which bordered on the pathological. It created for him periods of unbearable solitude. He constantly sought out other people with whom he hoped he would be compatible, both intellectually and personally. But when those he selected to fill these needs disappointed him, either by being too demanding or too critical, his initial response was to fall into a deep depression. Eventually, his depression evolved into aggressive, and sometimes virulent, counterattack. Three revealing examples are provided by his relationships with Ottoline Morrell, D.H. Lawrence, and Ludwig Wittgenstein.

Perhaps because he was always sexually attracted to Ottoline Morrell, his frequent anger and frustration with her tended to quickly diminish. After their disagreements, they would continue on as if there had never been a problem. Towards D.H. Lawrence, his initial respect and awe turned to dislike and disgust. No other person had an ability equal to that of Wittgenstein for upsetting Russell and throwing him into a slump. While he never ceased to be awed by Wittgenstein's genius, Russell did, in later years, express doubts about Wittgenstein's so-called "ordinary language" approach to philosophy.

In the end, the person with the greatest influence on Russell was Ottoline Morrell. Russell's autobiography credits her with having inaugurated in him a rejuvenation.[4] They met and fell for one another almost immediately. She was overwhelmed by his intellectual powers. In her diary, she claims to have never meet anyone more attractive, though disarmingly penetrating in judgment, than Russell. She notes that an acquaintance had described him as "The Day of Judgment." For his part, Russell was so taken with her that he tried for several years to persuade her to leave her husband, Philip Morrell, and to marry him. Although she never succumbed to Russell's entreaties to leave her husband, she remained Russell's friend and confidant until her death.

The relationship between Russell and Ottoline produced a prodigious amount of correspondence between them. It is an invaluable source of information concerning Russell's character and personality, as well as his feelings about many of this century's leading writers, political figures, and intellectuals. It is also a record of his many complicated liaisons with various women. In the afterglow of their own passionate love affair, Russell, doubtlessly motivated at times by his efforts to inspire Ottoline's jealousy, described to her his numerous and varying passions and entanglements with other woman. These revelations rarely had the desired effect.

Only when Ottoline thought she might lose Russell's affection would she "affect" jealousy. At one point, while visiting and lecturing in America, Russell was so frustrated by Ottoline's indifference to him as a lover that he became intimately involved with a young woman. Her name was Helen Dudley, and he wrote to Ottoline about their involvement. He succeeded in resurrecting Ottoline's interest in him by these means. But he went further, and asked Miss Dudley to join him in England, and eventually to marry him. She did come to England, but by that time he was completely indifferent to her. She was terribly hurt by his rejection of her, and continued to harass him. Unbelievably, he managed to talk Ottoline into letting Helen Dudley live with her. On one occasion, while Ottoline was visiting Russell, Helen appeared at the door, and begged Russell to let her in. He refused, and she beat on the door. Ottoline claims in her journal to have been distressed by this state of affairs. But her letters to Russell reveal that she was in fact sexually and emotionally aroused by the whole tawdry business. Helen finally gave up and returned home to America. Later in life, Russell tried to excuse his behavior towards her as being the result of the shock he felt at England's having entered the First World War. He claimed that had this event not intervened, he might well have married her. His correspondence with Ottoline at the time tells, unfortunately, a different and much less self-serving story.

Psychologically, Russell was haunted by feelings of alienation from other humans. He was often lonely and insecure. He vacillated between being elated by the conviction that he was an important thinker, even that he would be remembered as one of history's greatest thinkers, and being tormented by self doubts. On one occasion, he is reputed to have pointed to the busts of the great thinkers displayed along the corridors of the library at Trinity College, and to have claimed that his bust would someday join those already on display.

On occasion, he would confess to his current love interest that he was contemplating, or had contemplated at various times in his life, suicide. Although, it likely that many of these confessions were done for dramatic affect, meant to disarm and endear himself to the subject of his affection, it was, no doubt, something which he did at times take seriously. And it explains, at least in part, why he took seriously questions about the meaning of life.

Whatever may have been his faults, Russell is someone whose bust deserves to be among those displayed at Trinity College. He was a great thinker, and a great man. While his faults were no greater than most, his virtues were. He had intellectual talent, a passion for ideas, immense curiosity, a desire to understand the universe and mankind's place in it, a hatred of warfare, and the courage to go to jail for what he believed. These are just some of his many virtues. It was his intellectual virtues which set him apart, however. It is now time to examine the results he achieved because of them.

Endnotes

[1] Russell (1943) p. 12.

[2] Moore (1952) p. 13.

[3] See Kolak (1998) for a new translation of, and commentary on the *Tractatus*. Kolak succeeds in making the *Tractatus* readable for today's students.

[4] Russell (1968) p. 3.

II
Logic, Mathematics, Philosophy and Reality

Russell's efforts regarding the nature and development of modern logic were not as innovative as those of Leibniz, Pearce, Boole, Cantor, Peano, or Frege, but he was able to take what they had achieved and, with the help of Whitehead, develop a simplified formal technique. This technique included significant contributions of Russell's own, and it provided the means for substantially clarifying, developing and expressing the combined innovations of those whose work preceded him. He first set out his ideas in *The Principles of Mathematics*, and then he and Whitehead collaborated to produce *Principia Mathematica*.

In the preface to *Principia Mathematica* Russell informs us that their original intention was to publish it as part II of *The Principles of Mathematics*. It outgrew this intention, and was instead published as an independent work in three volumes. In *The Principles of Mathematics*, he attempted to prove that when we analyze mathematics, we bring it all back to logic. He had attempted to develop a logic through which he could derive the whole of mathematics--a logic involving the fewest possible number of definitions and axioms. His attempts were superseded by the success he and Whitehead had in the *Principia*. They succeeded in producing there a richer and more powerful logic than any of its predecessors. Their success demonstrated, as far as they and many of their contemporaries were concerned, the continuity of logic and mathematics. Logic and metaphysics were also inseparable for Russell. In the "Philosophy of Logical Atomism," he claims to be explicating "a certain kind of logical doctrine, and on the basis of this a certain kind of metaphysic."[1] He considered philosophy to be the best means available for us to discover the truth about the world in which we find ourselves. As was pointed out in the introduction, his reductionism and commitment to Descartes' "Method of Doubt," are inherent in his conception of philosophy as the best means for understanding the universe and ourselves. Like Descartes, he believed that only by subjecting our beliefs to critical scrutiny, and by breaking the complex down to its simplest parts, can we attain true beliefs. The Wittgenstein of the *Tractatus* shared, to a large extent, this conception of philosophy, but was led as a result of this very approach to recognize the limitations of philosophy. This recognition eventually led him to reject the views which he and Russell had shared. His critique of their joint efforts comprises the essence of his highly influential later work *Philosophical Investigations*. In this chapter, I will explicate the results of Russell's application of the method in question, as well as how Wittgenstein's work relates to Russell.

Russell's views concerning the nature and relevance of philosophy, his metaphilosophy, cannot be separated from his metaphysics. For Russell, it is of the essence of philosophy to give an account of the nature of things, and the best way to do so is to apply the method he helped to originate, namely logical analysis. For Russell, philosophy is essentially logic. In his seminal work *Our Knowledge of the External World* he devotes the whole of the second chapter, "Logic as the essence of Philosophy," to this thesis. He begins this chapter by explaining what he means by the word 'logic.' His does this because the word in question has seldom been used, even by philosophers, to mean the same thing. He looks at and criticizes the views of Aristotle, the scholastics, Bacon, Galileo, Mill, Hegel, and the modern logicians, Peano, Boole, and Frege. He summarizes his findings thus:

> Logic, we may say, consists of two parts. The first part investigates what propositions are and what forms they may have; this part enumerates the different kinds of atomic propositions, of molecular propositions, of general propositions, and so on. The second part consists of

supremely general propositions, which assert the truth of all propositions of certain forms.[2] This second part emerges as pure mathematics, whose propositions all turn out, on analysis to be such general formal truths. The first part, which merely enumerates forms, is the more difficult, and philosophically the more important: and it is the recent progress in this first part, more than anything else, that has rendered a truly scientific discussion of many philosophical problems possible.[3]

In "The Philosophy of Logical Atomism" Russell claims that the kind of philosophy he wishes to "advocate" is one which forced itself upon him "in the course of thinking about the philosophy of mathematics". According to Russell, "when we analyze mathematics we bring it all back to logic,...a certain kind of logical doctrine, and on the basis of this a certain kind of metaphysic."[4]

No one offers a better and more concise exegesis of Russell's program than does J. O. Urmson who says about Russell that he:

considered that a logic from which the whole of mathematics with all of its complexities can be derived must be an adequate skeleton... of a language capable of expressing all that can be accurately said at all.... he came to think that the world would have the structure of this logic, whose grammar was so perfect, unlike that of the misleading natural languages. As the logic had individual variables in its vocabulary, so the world would contain a variety of particulars, the names of which would be constants, to replace, as extra-logical vocabulary, these variables; as the logic required only extensional, truth- functional, connective between its elementary propositions, so the world would consist of independent, extensionally connected facts; as the techniques of logic could define and thus make theoretically superfluous the more complex and abstruse concepts of mathematics, so, by the application of the same techniques the less concrete items of the furniture of heaven and earth,...could be defined and eliminated.[5]

The *truth functional* approach to logic which Russell and Whitehead clarified, and elaborated in Principia. became the model for most logic texts written within this century. Any one of these texts can be consulted for a detailed presentation of it. However, since a familiarity with truth functional logic is necessary for an understanding of what follows, I will provide a brief account of its essentials.

Logic is a formal technique for the analysis and evaluation of discourse. Discourse can be broken down into the simple and the complex. The simplest kind of assertion is the attribution of some simple characteristic or property to a simple object, for example "That is a small dab of red paint." I complicate matters only slightly if I say about the same dab of paint that it is not white. Less simple, but relatively speaking, still quite simple are such claims as: "George is a bachelor;" "It is cold;" or "Finn is in New York." The difference between these claims and the one about the dab of paint is simply that their subjects are more complex. A dab of paint is far less complex than a person, or a state of nature, and each of these less complex than a planet or a galaxy. Frequently, however, we wish to say things like: (a) "That one is white, and this one is red," (b) "Either it cold, or it is sunny," (c) "If Finn is in New York, he is not having any fun," (d) "My father is dead, but my mother is alive," (e) "Being a bachelor is the same as being an unmarried male of a marriageable age." These latter assertions involve combining the former kinds of assertion. Their complexity is *relational*, but not *structural*.

The assertions (a) through (e) can in fact be used to illustrate a variety of relational complexities. In the case of (a), one is saying or claiming both that one thing is white and that another thing is red. Logicians refer to this form of combining simple assertions as *conjunction*. It can be distinguished from (b) on the grounds that, in (b), one is only committed to its being cold, or its being sunny, but not both. This relation is commonly designated as *disjunction*. In the case of (c), one is asserting that from the fact that one is in New York, it follows that one is not having any fun. This relation is generally designated as *implication*. To assert (d) is to assert an identity between being a bachelor and being an unmarried male of marriageable age. This relation is called *equivalence*.

These relational complexities are said to be "truth functional," which simply means that their truth or falsity is a function of the truth or falsity of their components. If one dab of paint is white, and another is red, then it follows that what is alleged by (a) is true, but if either

15

dab of paint lacks the color attributed to it, then it is false that one is white and the other is red. And, of course, if neither have the color it is alleged to have, (a) is false. All of which can be generalized and displayed by what is called a truth table matrix, an innovation of Wittgenstein's. What has been illustrated by the case involving the two simple assertions, "It is white," and "It is red," can be generalized regarding any two such assertions and expressed in terms of variables. Variables are place holders, and in this context they are place holders for simple assertions. If we use 'p' and 'q' as variables, and let 'p' stand in for the first of our assertions, or conjuncts, and 'q' for the second conjunct, we can use 'p and q' to symbolize any conjunctive sentence involving two conjuncts. If we also let 'T' stand for "is true" and 'F' for "is false," we can provide the following truth table matrix for conjunction. In the case of (b), we can likewise generalize and claim that if either of our simple components, disjuncts, are true then (b) is true, and that (b) would be false only if both are false. The matrix for disjunction is displayed on the right- hand side below:

p and q			Either p or q		
Row 1. T	T	T	1. T	T	T
Row 2. T	F	F	2. T	T	F
Row 3. F	F	T	3. F	T	F
Row 4. F	F	F	4. F	F	F

What these truth table matrixes display are the truth possibilities which exist for two simple assertions, formalized by 'p' and 'q'. If one has more conjuncts or disjuncts, the number of rows needed to display the truth possibilities will have to be increased. Since there are only two truth values to consider "true" and "false," a formula can be provided to tell us how many rows we will need to exhaust all the truth possibilities for a conjunction involving any given number of conjuncts or disjuncts. Given that 'n' is the number of conjuncts or disjuncts, and '2' is the number of possible truth values, that formula is 2n. A conjunctive assertion involving three conjuncts will require eight rows to display all its truth possibilities.

Although, I have used the symbols 'p' and 'q' to stand in place of simple propositions or statements, I have retained the English expressions for the relations: 'and;' 'either ...or;' and 'not'. They can also be replaced by symbols. Various notations have been introduced to accomplish this task. The notation devised by Russell, based upon Peano's, uses the period for conjunction, so that, for example, 'p and q' when fully symbolized becomes 'p . q.' Other symbols were introduced for the other relations, but I will continue to use English for all of them. Negation is also truth functional. If p is true, then not-p will have to be false, but if p is false then not-p will have to be true. Since we have only one variable, only two rows are required to provide the matrix for *negation*.

p   not p

Row 1. T   F
Row 2. F   T

Implication, or the *conditional*, and equivalence, or the *bi-conditional*, are not so easily analyzed. The latter can be defined in terms of the former plus conjunction as: p implies q, and q implies p, but the analysis of implication generates difficulties-- difficulties which carry over to the bi-conditional. In the case of conjunction, the truth values for the conjunction of p and q can be deduced for each row given the values under p, and those under q. If p is false, or q is false, or both are false, then the conjunction of p and q is false-- rows 2, 3, and 4 above. But look at what happens when we try to fill in the values for the truth table matrix for p implies q.

p implies q

Row 1   T   ?   T
Row 2   T   F   F
Row 3   F   ?   T
Row 4   F   ?   F

Given that p implies q means that if p is true then q is true, it follows that p cannot be true and q be false, and thus row 2 would have to be false. But from the mere fact that both p and q are true (Row 1) one cannot deduce either that p implies q, or that p does not imply q. It is true that I am both wearing loafers and a necktie, but clearly having on the one piece of apparel hardly implies having on the other. I just slipped off my loafers. Row 2 is now the case, which means that the

17

one thing does not imply the other. Yet, obviously, from the fact that two assertions are both true, it does not follow that one does not imply the other. Its true both that my German Shepherd is a dog, and that she is an animal, and the former does imply the latter. Nor does it follow that if p is false, and q is true (Row 3), that anything can be deduced regarding whether or not p implies q. Since we have already determined that Row 2 is possible, we already know that wearing the loafers does not imply wearing the necktie. But would the possibility displayed as Row 3 show that p does not imply q? No, my horse is not a dog, but he is an animal, but this does not show, nor could anything, that being a dog does not imply being an animal. One might think, however, that if both p and q are false (Row 4) one could deduce that p does not imply q. Not true. Although x is a dog does imply that x is an animal, it is false both that my pen is either a dog or an animal. Are we to conclude from these considerations that implication and the bi-conditional cannot be defined truth functionally? Although it is clear that the conventional meaning of the word 'implies' does not lend itself to a truth functional analysis, that fact need not deter the logician. All that is actually required of a truth functional relation is that it be defined truth functionally. This is what Russell and Whitehead did in *Principia*. They defined 'p implies q' as "Either not p or q."[6]   To distinguish this sense of 'implies', from the conventional one they referred to it as "material implication." This definition is not altogether arbitrary. It fits to some extent our standard conception of implication. We can understand and accept the idea that another way of saying that being a dog implies being also an animal, is to say that either it is not a dog, or it is an animal. The truth table analysis for 'either not p or q' is:

either not p or q
*
Row 1. F T T T
Row 2. F T F F
Row 3. T F T T
Row 4. T F T F
*

The column marked both at the top and at the bottom with '*' provides the truth functional analysis for the statement in question, which is derived from the values under not p, and those under q when we follow the matrix previously provided for disjunction. That matrix reveals that we get an F for "either p or q" only when both disjuncts are F. In our present case, the first disjunct is not p (which is F whenever p is T) and the second disjunct is q. It is only in Row 2 that not p is F when q is also F. In the other Rows one or the other or both not p and q are true. We can now define material implication as being truth functionally equivalent to "either not p or q," and replace the question mark in Rows 1, 3, and 4 with a T. This is precisely the procedure followed by Russell and Whitehead in Principia. The reason they do it this way is that they take alternation and negation to be the primitives of their truth functional account and define the other relations or operations in terms of them. One could, however, designate conjunction and negation as primitives and define the other relations in terms of them. Implication or the conditional would then be defined as "it is not the case both that p is true, and that q is false. The truth functional analysis for this expression is:

It is not the case that (p and not q)

		#			*		
Row 1	T		T	F	F	T	
Row 2	F		T	T	T	F	
Row 3	T		F	F	F	T	
Row 4	T		F	F	T	F	
		#			*		

The column marked with the '*' both at the top and at the bottom is the truth table for the expression within the parenthesis, which is derived from the matrix for "p and q," which yields a T only when both p and q are T (Row 2). The final analysis for the full expression is given under the column marked with an '#', which is derived from the matrix for negation, as it is the negation of the values marked by the '*'. Wherever you get a T under the 'and' (the column marked by an '*') you get an F under its negation (the column marked by '#'), and vice versa. Notice that the values under the negation or the column # are the same as those assigned to implication, as well as those we derived for "either not p or q". What follows from this is that material implication can be defined as simply an abbreviation of "It is not the case that (p and not q)." In other words we could always symbolize any claim that one thing implies another in terms of negation and conjunction, the conventional meanings of which lend themselves to a straight forward truth functional analysis. Remember that if p is true, then q must be true is just another way of saying that you cannot have p true and q false-- it is not the case that (p and not q). The bi-conditional or equivalence can now be truth functionally defined in terms of material implication and conjunction as "p materially implies q and q materially implies q," all of which can be spelled out in terms of negation and conjunction as "It is not the case that (p and not q) and it is not the case that (q and not p)."

Armed with this basic understanding of symbolic logic, we are now in a position to better appreciate Russell's metaphysics--logical atomism. For Russell, the philosopher's task is to provide through a rigorous application of logic or the analytical method an account of the world of science and daily life. To do so the philosopher must determine what are the ultimate constituents of the world. Through analysis he has to reduce the apparent complexities of the world into their simplest components. Logical atomism was the result of a joint endeavor by Russell and the early Wittgenstein. And although there are significant differences in the kind of account each gave, they shared a common understanding as regards how this should be done, and what kinds of problems it was meant to address and resolve.

At the outset of "The Philosophy of Logical Atomism," Russell explains that his approach is "atomistic" in as much as the world consists of many separate things, and does not, as the Hegelians insist, consist merely in phases and unreal divisions of a single reality. He explains that the atoms are "logical" rather than empirical and physical atoms. They are revealed by logical and not chemical analysis. The atoms are two kinds, particulars-- "little paths of color, sounds, momentary things"--and predicates or relations. Logical analysis is said to be the only way for us to learn the truth about the world in which we find ourselves.

Russell regards our common everyday beliefs and the assertions we make based upon them to be "fearfully vague," but logical analysis can replace these vague and imprecise everyday beliefs with beliefs which are inherently clear and precise. The expression of precise and unambiguous beliefs or propositions requires a language which, unlike ordinary language, is constructed from the outset for this purpose. Such a language is regarded as "ideal," but is also a reality for Russell. He believed that he and Whitehead had provided the rudiments of such a language in *Principia Mathematica*. All that remains to be accomplished is to delineate, and describe or develop, principles upon the basis of which one could generate the vocabulary for this language.

In order to arrive at a language free from the vagueness which characterizes natural languages, we must, according to Russell, provide terms the meanings of which are strictly fixed and determinate. Before proceeding to specify exactly what characteristics these terms will have to possess, Russell explains what he means by a fact. Facts are what they are no matter what we may think about them. They are independent of our beliefs about them. They are required to provide content to our beliefs. They are expressed by our claims about the world. They render what we say to be either true or false. They are expressed by whole sentences, not by names. Facts are expressed "when we say that a certain thing has a certain property, or that it has a certain relation to another thing; but the thing which has the property or the relation is not what I call a fact."[7]

There are, according to Russell, two kinds of fact. There are particular facts, and there are general facts. A specific sense datum's being white is his example of a particular fact, all humans being mortal is his example of a general fact, and he cautions us against supposing that one could "describe the world completely by means of particular facts alone."[8]   He offers a proof of this contention. He asks us to suppose that we have listed all the particular facts in the universe. Would we then, he asks, have a complete list of all existent facts. No, says Russell. Our list would not be complete because it leaves out the fact that it is complete. In order to complete the list we would have to add the general fact that all particular facts are contained on our list.

This argument, which stuck Russell as obvious, is by no means indisputable. Suppose I make out a list of all the various particular items which are to be found in the top middle drawer of my desk. Having completed that task, it would correct to say that all the particular things in that drawer have been chronicled, but it would be equally correct to say that this particular list is complete. Whether or not I choose to describe this state of affairs by saying "This list is complete," or by saying "All the items in my middle desk drawer have been listed," makes no difference what-so-ever.

But, in Russell's defense, could we not say that "This list is complete," really means that "All the items in my middle desk drawer have been listed"? One could, of course, say this, but how would one defend it? No principle of logic or math could decide this issue because it is not a deductive matter. Empirically speaking, is it any less defensible to say that the latter really means the former?

Russell proceeds by distinguishing between those things which are logically complex, and those things which are logically simple in order to facilitate the reduction of the complex to the simple, and eventually to the most simple elements, namely, particulars. Our common sense assumption that most of the objects to which we attach proper names, for example, Socrates, Rumania, Twelfth Night, Piccadilly, are actually complex objects, is, he asserts, mistaken. We wrongly assume that such objects as these are "complex systems bound together in some kind of unity, that sort of a unity that leads us to the bestowal of a simple appellation." For Russell, such complex objects as these do not actually exist. He claims that they are simply "logical fictions."9

Take the statement "Piccadilly is a pleasant street." Is there any single constituent in the fact that this statement describes which can be said to correspond to the name 'Piccadilly'? The answer to this question is, according to Russell, that there is no single constituent of this fact, simple or complex, which could be referred to by this expression. Although, 'Piccadilly' "on the face of it, is the name for a certain portion of the earth's surface," to define 'Piccadilly' one would, we are told, "have to define it as a series of classes of material entities."

In other words, if I asked you to tell me to what does the name 'Piccadilly' refer, you would probably say that in addition to some portion of the earth's surface it refers to the pavement, the lampposts, and some specifiable set of buildings, presently occupied by a specifiable number of shops, theaters, etc. And if I wanted you to be more specific, you could provide me with a description of each of these various enterprises. Such a description would be a description in terms of classes of objects. However, this set of enterprises, as well as the lampposts, streets, etc. are transitory--what is there today is not precisely what was there a year ago. Lampposts get destroyed and are replaced by others. Businesses fail or lose their leases, and are replaced by others. This is why Russell says that we are talking about series of classes--classes the members of which are in flux.

For Russell, abstractions like classes do not refer to any object, and so they are unreal--logical fictions. If I asked you how many hounds are owned by the Potomac Hunt, you would count them. If I asked you how many different hound colors you observed as you counted the hounds, you would, if you were a hound aficionado, say there are two classes, lemon and whites, and tricolors, but there are no black and tans. If I asked you to point to or pet one of the tricolors, it would be easy for you to do so, but if I asked you to point to or pet the class of tricolors, you would be at a loss to do so. You might say that classes do not exist the way that dogs do. Classes are abstractions. You can pen up all the tri-colors, but how would you pen up or otherwise confine a class? Russell treats human beings the same way he treats Piccadilly. For him, Socrates is nothing more than the series of his experiences, and as such, a logical fiction. But as Kurt Godel points out, what Russell means by the term 'exits' is not what we usually mean by it. What Russell means when he says that these things do not exist is, according to Godel, "only that we have no direct experience of them."[10]

In an earlier essay, "On Denoting," which I will cover in the next chapter, Russell considered 'Apollo' to be a disguised description. In that work he distinguished between proper names like 'Scott,' and disguised descriptions like 'Apollo' and by doing so left us with the impression that the meaning of the former were the objects to which they referred.[11] Now he tells us that all ordinary proper names are disguised descriptions, and that we must distinguish between ordinary proper names, and logically proper names. Logically proper names are said to mean or refer to simple objects or particulars, which he contrasts with facts. For Russell, facts are *genuinely* complex objects. About them he says:

> Facts are... plainly something you have to take account of if you are going to give a complete account of the world. You cannot   do that by merely enumerating the particular things that are in it: you must also mention the relations of these things, and their   properties, and so forth, all of which are facts, so that the facts certainly belong to an account of the objective world, and facts do seem much more clearly complex and much more not capable of being explained away than things like Socrates...[12]

Russell continues his analysis by defining the word 'proposition' which he defines as being composed of symbols, symbols which "we must understand in order to understand the proposition." Excluding the logical components of propositions ('and,' 'or,' 'not,' 'if...then,' 'if and only if,' etc.), Russell defines "the meanings of the symbols" composing propositions as "the components of facts."[13] By defining propositions in this way, he is defining them as most philosophers would define sentences, specifically sentence *types*, not sentence *tokens*. Sentence tokens are the actual physical instances of the specific sentence types. 'This is white,' and 'This is white' are said to be different tokens or *instantiations* of the same type. The proposition or sentence type 'This is white' has as its meaning the fact that it describes. The meaning of 'this' is the thing that is white, and the meaning of 'white' is the whiteness of the thing referred to by 'this.'

Russell proceeds by postulating a hierarchy of facts starting with the simplest and proceeding to the more complex. The simplest sort of facts are, according to Russell, "those which consist in the possession of a quality by some particular thing," for example, what is referred to by the proposition 'This is white'. Next simplest, would be referred to by such sentences or propositions as 'This is to the left of that,' followed by such facts as those referred to by such sentences as 'A gives B to C.' Such facts are referred to as 'monadic,' 'dyadic,' 'triadic,' 'tetradic,' etc., depending upon whether the relation involves one, two, three, four, or n number of terms. This whole hierarchy is said by Russell to "constitute" what he calls *atomic facts*--the simplest sort of fact. The sentences describing these facts are defined as *atomic propositions*. And every atomic fact is said to involve one component, namely a monadic, dyadic, triadic, etc. relation, and the terms of the relation, which are particulars. In atomic propositions, the symbols expressing the relations are said to be *predicates*, and the symbols expressing or standing for particulars are *logically proper names*.

Molecular propositions are composed of atomic propositions. Molecular propositions, for example, 'This is white and that is red,' 'This is red or it is purple,' 'If this is white, it is colored,' etc. are said to be *truth functional*. To say that they are truth functional is to say, as was explained in our study of symbolic logic, that their truth values are functions of the truth values of their constituent parts. If it is true that a given simple object is white and another one is red, then 'This is white and that is red' is also true.

Propositions like 'Russell believes that this is white,' which seems to consist of two simpler parts, namely, 'This is White,' and 'Russell believes that it is white,' are not, Russell cautions, truth functional since the truth of the proposition in question is not determined by its parts. The truth or falsity of 'This is white,' is irrelevant to the truth of whether or not Russell believes it. For this reason beliefs cannot be analyzed as two term relations.

Failure to recognize that belief statements cannot be analyzed as two term relations has, declares Russell, "vitiated almost everything that has hitherto been written on the theory of knowledge, making the problem of error insoluble and the difference between belief and perception inexplicable." Russell considers such discoveries as this, which result from the utilization of the method of logical analysis, to be evidence that "this new logic" can be regarded as the same kind of advance which "Galileo introduced into physics, making it possible at last to see what kinds of problems may be capable of solution, and what kinds must be abandoned as beyond human powers."[14]

As we have seen, Russell places great importance upon the concept of a particular. He defines the expression 'particular' as "a term of relation in an atomic fact,"-- not exactly a pithy explanation. Why not provide us with an example? Russell's response to this kind of request is baffling. He says:

> The whole question of what particulars you actually find in the real world is a purely empirical one which does not interest the logician as such. The logician as such never gives instances, because it is one of the tests of a logical proposition that you need not know anything whatsoever about the real world in order to understand it.[15]

He does relent, however, by claiming a couple of pages later that the only words of ordinary language which can serve as proper names and name particulars are such words as 'this' and 'that,' and as he proceeds to explain their use he does provide an example of a particular:

> One can use 'this' as a name to stand for a particular with which one is acquainted at the moment... It is only when you use 'this' quite strictly to stand for an actual object of sense [sense datum] that it is really a proper name. And in that it has a very odd property for a proper name, that it seldom means the same thing two moments running and it does not mean the same thing to the speaker as it does to the hearer.[16]

The example which Russell utilizes to illustrate what he means by a particular is any individual audience member's sensation of a chalk spot which he put on a blackboard for them to observe. It is here that Russell sows the seeds for his future refutation at the hands of Wittgenstein, his most valued protégé. In the question period which followed this lecture, a Mr. Neville asks "If the proper name of a thing, a 'this,' varies from instant to instant, how is it possible to make any argument?[17]   In other words, if Russell is right, every argument involving particulars would commit the fallacy of equivocation. Whenever a word is used in a premise with a meaning different from the meaning it would have to have to warrant the conclusion, we have an instance of such a fallacy. For example, "Since good steaks are rare, it follows that they must be hard to find." As we have seen, for Russell the meaning of a 'this,' or any other name for a particular, is the object to which it refers.[18]   Since the object referred to by the 'this' in the example which Russell has provided varies so frequently, and is, as Russell concedes, ambiguous, will not any argument involving particulars, of necessity, be invalid? Russell responds to this objection by claiming that:

> You can keep 'this' going for about a minute or two. I made that dot and talked about it for some little time... If you argue quickly, you can get some little way before it is finished. I think things last for a finite time, a matter of some seconds or minutes or whatever it may happen to be.[19]

In the first place, Russell blurs the distinction between the actual spot which he put on the blackboard and each individual audience member's sensation of it. You can, of course, continue to talk about the spot on the board for a great many minutes, even hours, days, months, etc., depending upon how long you are willing to do so. But Russell asked each member of his audience to focus upon his own sensation of it. If one blinks, or has his attention diverted for even a micro-second, then that person would no longer be referring to the same thing or having the same sensation. And for that reason, it is, at best, extremely difficult to imagine how anyone could complete an argument concerning one's own sensation of the spot without equivocating. But it is worse than this. How, for example, does one know that he has succeeded in focusing upon the same sense-datum throughout the course of his efforts to state a valid argument? To what could one appeal to establish that one had succeeded? Can we even understand what would be the difference between actually succeeding in, and only being under the impression that one is succeeding in, focusing upon the same sensation? Not according to Wittgenstein who argues that in such cases one has "no criterion of correctness. One would like to say: whatever is going to seem right to me is right. And that only means that here we can't talk   about 'right'."

This is a shortened version of Wittgenstein's famous "private language argument," a misnomer, as it is literally an anti-private language argument.[20]   One consequence of this argument of Wittgenstein's is that communication would be impossible to accomplish with Russell's ideal language--not exactly a desirable characteristic for any language much less an ideal one! If, when I say "It is white," I am referring to my own (private) sensory impression, and you, when you utter the same words, are referring to your own sensory impression, we cannot be talking about the same thing--what I mean is different from what you mean. If that were not bad enough, what is worse is that I cannot even talk to myself. According to Russell, even if I blink, that would cause the contents of my sensory field to be different. By the time I have said to myself that the object of my experience is white, I *may* not be talking about what I mean to be talking about. Can I ever be sure whether or not I am thinking or talking about what I mean to be thinking or talking about? No, not if what I am thinking or talking about is a private sensory impression.

No analysis of Russell's logical atomism would be complete without coverage of one of Russell's most ingenious and subtle theories--the theory of types. It is not an easy theory to explain, even Whitehead expressed frustration regarding it, and many different opinions exist among logicians and mathematicians regarding its nature. I will try to produce an account of it which is consistent with my understanding of its various expositions both by Russell and others.

In *Principia*, Russell and Whitehead attempted to reduce mathematics to logic by reducing numbers to classes. Understood in this way it would seem that a class could be understood *extensionally* as simply the conjunction of a collection of objects. Such reductionism is, however, hampered by the paradoxes which are engendered by the concept of classes. What about those classes of objects which have infinite numbers as members? What would a conjunction of such a class look like? Would it not have to be an infinite conjunction? And what are those objects which make up the null class? Are they non-objects? Worse than this, however, is the fact that since any class of objects n can be divided into two sets of objects $2n$, it follows that even in the case where n is infinite, $2n$ is greater than n. So if we assume that n is the total number of things, and include within it the total number of things which can be composed from it, we arrive at the self-contradictory result that the total number of things that exist is greater than their totality. To provide a better understanding of this paradox, Russell asks us to consider a class with just three members, a, b, and c. The first selection we are asked to make is the selection of no terms, then of a alone, followed by b alone, and then c alone. Then we are asked to select bc, cab, ab, and abc. We now have 8 selections, which can be determined ahead of such inductive procedures via the formula, $2n$ where n is the number of terms--the same formula we used to determine the number of rows needed for constructing truth tables. "Generally speaking" says Russell, "if you have n terms you can make $2n$ selections." From which he concludes "So you find that the total number of things in the world is not so great as the number of classes that can be made up out of those things." And, that we can construct on these grounds, "a perfectly precise arithmetical proof that there are *fewer* things in heaven or earth than are dreamt of in *our* philosophy."[21]

Such considerations led Russell to give up the idea that classes could be analyzed extensionally, and to treat them instead *intensionally* --as classes of objects satisfying or instantiating propositional functions. The class of humans is just that collection of objects which yields true values for the function "x is human."

Russell can now eliminate classes by reducing statements about classes to statements about corresponding propositional functions. But this kind of reductionism generates serious difficulties of its own. There is a serious problem concerning classes which are, and those which are not, members of themselves. In the case of ordinary classes like the class of dogs, one would likely say that this is a class which is not a member of itself--classes are not dogs. Consider, however, the class composed of all such classes, namely, those classes which do not contain themselves as members. Now let us ask about this class as we did about the class of dogs, does it contain itself as a member? Paradoxically, if we suppose that it *does*, it follows that as such it is one of those classes that *does not* contain itself as a member. If, on the other hand, we assume that it *does not* contain itself as a member, then it *is* one of those classes that does not contain itself as a member. In either case we contradict ourselves.

Another paradox which Russell considers is the paradox of

Epimenides, the Cretan who claimed that all Cretans are liars. Russell recasts it as a question "if a man makes the statement 'I am lying,' is he lying or not?" If he is lying, then that is what he says he is doing, so he is telling the truth and not lying. But if he is telling the truth, then he is lying, and so not telling the truth.22

To overcome such paradoxes as these Russell devised the theory of types. He originally introduced in an 1908 article entitled "Mathematical Logic as based upon the Theory of Types." He refined it in *Principia Mathematica*, and explicated it further in "The Philosophy of Logical Atomism." In *Principia*, he explicates the notion of a propositional function by saying that it is "something which contains a variable *x*, and expresses a *proposition* as soon as a value is assigned to x." He also claims that a propositional function "is what ambiguously denotes some one of a certain totality, namely the values of the function." From which it follows, according to Russell, that "this totality cannot contain any members which involve the function, since if it did it would contain members involving the totality, which, by the vicious-circle principle, no totality can do."23

This contention of Russell's, that a propositional function cannot contain itself as a member, the so-called "simple theory of types,"24 provides immediate solution to the paradox about the class of classes which are not members of themselves. What follows if one adopts the simple theory of types, is that the question whether it is true or false that such a class does contain itself as a member is itself revealed to be meaningless. The question would be as senseless as asking if a full marble bag contains itself.

The person claiming that he is lying will have to say what type of liar he is. If he claims "I am asserting a false proposition of the first type", then he will be, according to Russell , asserting a proposition of the second type. So, since he is not asserting a proposition of the first type, he remains a liar, and there is no contradiction. "Similarly", according to Russell, "if he said he was asserting a false proposition of the 30,000th type, that would be a statement of the 30,001st type, so he would still be a liar."25

The theory of types is, as Reichenbach recognized, the bedrock principle underlying the language/meta-language distinction. Although Tarski is often credited with introducing this distinction, it was, according to Reichenbach, "simply an extension of the theory of types to a theory of levels of language... anticipated by Russell himself..."26

when, in his Introduction to Wittgenstein's *Tractatus*, he says:

> ... every language has, as Mr. Wittgenstein says, a structure concerning which, in the language, nothing can be said, but there may be another language dealing with the structure of the first language, and having itself a new structure, and that to this hierarchy of languages there may be no limit.[27]

What the object language/meta-language distinction involves can best be understood by focusing upon the difference between talking about objects on the one hand, and talking about talk itself on the other. My dog is a German Shepherd. What I stated, call it S, with the previous sentence is a fact *about* my dog Suzy. Suppose now I state that my statement about Suzy was true. With this last statement, call it MS, I am saying something *about* my previous statement S, and *not about* my dog Suzy. As in the case of the theory of types, the recognition of meta-languages forces one to acknowledge the existence of a hierarchy of meta-languages. I can, for example, say that MS is true, call this statement MS1, and this would be a statement about MS. This last statement, MS1, is a statement about a statement, MS, about a statement, S, about a dog. To state that MS1 is true, call it MS2, is to make a statement about a statement, MS1, about a statement, MS, about a statement, S, about Suzy. On this pattern we can imagine what is, in principle, a infinite set of possible sentences. Russell's theory of types, when interpreted to generate a hierarchy of meta-languages, can be used to solve various kinds of philosophical issues.

An example of its use to resolve a philosophical issue is its resolution of one of the major objections to positivism. According to positivists like Rudolph Carnap,[28] the meaning of a sentence is its method of verification, or:

> No proposition can be accepted as meaningful unless we understand how to verify it.

But, as positivism's critics were quick to point out, the verification principle itself is not subject to verification, so it must be meaningless. If, however, we interpret the principle as follows, we can rule out this form of objection.

No proposition about objects can be accepted as meaningful unless we understand how to verify it.

It is no longer self-referring. Interpreted in this way, it is a criterion of acceptability of propositions or statements about objects, and not a statement about objects. This is not to say that the verification principle is true or justifiable, only that it does not contain the seeds of its own destruction. It is not self-refuting. Other grounds would have to be provided in order to establish its acceptance.[29]

As noted previously, Wittgenstein eventually rejected his own and Russell's approach to philosophy. In the *Investigations*, he launches a lengthy critique of their joint endeavors, including logical atomism, and its offspring, logical positivism. I will explain Wittgenstein's critique at the end of the next chapter, after I have presented Russell's views on meaning and referring, views which Wittgenstein also attacks.

Endnotes

[1] Russell (1918) p. 178.

[2] By which Russell means what we commonly refer to as argument forms. He exemplifies the notion by use of "If anything has a certain property, and whatever has this property has another property, then the thing in question has the other property." (p. 51).

[3] Russell (1929) p. 52.

[4] Russell (1918) p. 298.

[5] Urmson (1956) p. 7.

[6] Russell and Whitehead, (1910) p. 7.

[7] Ibid., p. 302.

[8] Here as well as throughout the work under consideration Russell seems to be confusing "facts" with the expression of them through language. Descriptions are linguistic entities, facts are what are described.

[9] Russell (1918) p. 308.

[10] Godel (1944) p. 127.

[11] See below, pp. 33-36.

[12] Russell (1918) p. 309.

13 Ibid., p. 313.

14 Russell (1929) pp. 52-53.

15 Russell (1918) p. 315.

16 Ibid., p. 317.

17 Ibid., p. 318.

18 For a further discussion and another example of this kind of fallacy, see p. 53 of the present book.

19 Ibid., p. 318.

20 Wittgenstein (1958) Section 258, p. 92e.

21 Russell (1918) p. 363.

22 Ibid., p. 365.

23 Russell (1910) p. 39.

24 In contrast to the "ramified theory of types," which necessitated the introduction of the principle of reducibility, and which gave rise to difficulties into which we shall not venture. The reader interested in this issue should start with Reichenbach (1944) pp. 38- 39.

25 Russell (1918) pp. 364-367.

26 Reichenbach, H. (1944) p. 39.

27 Wittgenstein, L. (1922) *Tractatus Logico Philosophicus* (London: Routledge & Kegan Paul. LTD.) p. 23.

28 Carnap (1932).

29 For an effort to accomplish this end, as well as an extended analysis of this application of the theory of types understood in terms of the object-language/ meta-language distinction, see Odell/Zartman (1982).

III
Meaning and Language

In this chapter I will cover Russell's referential theory of meaning, his theory of descriptions, and his view that a formal language can be constructed to avoid the ambiguities inherent in natural languages. I will also explicate those views of P.F. Strawson which are widely believed to be the most telling critique of Russell's theory of descriptions. In conclusion, I will discuss those views Wittgenstein expresses in the Investigations, which are meant to cast serious doubt regarding Russell's approach to these topics. I will begin with an analysis of Russell's theory of descriptions, as presented in his 1903 work, "On Denoting," an essay which many philosophers regard as the wellspring of twentieth century analytic philosophy.

In "On Denoting," (1905) Russell confronts the topic of referring by posing three paradoxes, he refers to them as puzzles, which result because of inadequacies inherent in natural language. He claims, moreover, that these paradoxes provide a test for the adequacy of a philosophical theory of referring. He claims that such paradoxes serve the same purpose for logic that experiments do for science--they are tests. A theory of referring is, according to Russell, tested by its ability to resolve these paradoxes. He claims that his theory, the theory of descriptions, meets the challenge by offering solutions to all three.[1]

The first of these puzzles can be stated in the form of an argument, the first premise of which is the *principle of substitutivity*.

(P1) If terms 'a' and 'b' refer to the same thing then one of them can always be replaced by the other in any sentential context without change of truth value.

The second premise of the argument is an alleged historical fact about the curiosity of King George IV concerning Sir Walter Scott.

(P2) George IV wished to know whether Scott was the author of Waverly.

Premise three alleges a fact about English usage:

(P3) The expressions 'Scott' and 'the author of Waverly' refer to the same person.

On the basis of these three premises one can validly infer the following:

(C) George IV wished to know whether Scott was Scott.

This is not what George IV wanted to know. The conclusion is false, a fact which seems to undermine the very concept of "validity." To say that an argument is valid is to claim that it has a valid form. To say that it has a valid form is to claim that when its premises are true, its conclusion must be true. So, asks Russell, "Why is the conclusion false?"

The second puzzle is linked to the law of the excluded middle, which asserts that "either p or not p is true," or, to put it differently, contradictory propositions cannot both have the same truth value. Although this is a time honored and venerable principle of logic, Russell argues that there appear to be exceptions to it. Consider the following pair of contradictory sentences. Which one of them is true?

The present king of France is bald
The present king of France is not bald

According to Russell, since there is at present no king of France, it follows that nothing is both the king of France, and bald, tall, slender, intelligent, or anything else. To claim otherwise, as one does when one claims that he is bald, is to claim what is false. But what about the claim that he is not bald? According to the law of the excluded middle, it has to be true. But, by the same reasoning previously used to show that it is false that he is bald, it follows that it is also false that he is not bald. Because there is no present king of France, there cannot be anything which is both the present king of France and non-bald. The last of these paradoxes has to do with the inconsistency involved in denying the existence of anything. Consider the following:

(a) Apollo does not exist.

If one were to state the following three sentences, one would apparently be making true statements.

(1) (a) expresses a true proposition[2]
(2) (a) is about Apollo.
(3) (a) is *logically equivalent*[3] to the following sentence.[4]

(b) There is no such thing as Apollo.

But, claims Russell, they cannot all be consistently asserted, because if (1) and (3) are true, then (b) is true, and there is no such thing as Apollo, so (2) would have to false. On the other hand, if (2) is true, then (b) is false, and if (3) is true as well, then (1) would also have to be false. But if (2) and (1) are both true, then (3) will have to be false, since it would follow that (a) and (b) have different truth values.[5]

Russell's solutions to these puzzles derive from his theory of descriptions. The insight which motivates this theory is his recognition that we are seduced by ordinary language to treat all denoting expressions equally. We regard them all as names, and as such we interpret each one of them to refer to a specific object--that object being their meaning. In a proper logical language, an ideal language, we would never be tempted to do so. In such a language, all names would be logically proper names, which, as we saw in the last chapter, always refer to particulars.

According to Russell, denoting phrases, including 'the present king of England,' 'the present king of France,' 'some men,' 'all men,' 'the center of mass of the solar system at the first instant of the twentieth century,' unlike proper names, "never have any meaning in themselves." Instead they are, for Russell, *incomplete symbols*. In

Principia Mathematica, he defines the expression 'incomplete symbol' as "a symbol which is not supposed to have a meaning in isolation, but is only defined in certain context." He goes on to say:

> Whenever the grammatical subject of a proposition can be supposed not to exist without rendering the proposition meaningless, it is plain that the grammatical subject is not a proper name, i.e. not a name directly representing some object. Thus in all such cases, the proposition must be capable of being so analyzed that what was the grammatical subject shall have disappeared.[6]

In "On Denoting," Russell offers the following example as an illustration in the application of his theory of descriptions.

> The father of Charles II was executed.

Its analysis must, according to Russell, recognize that although we do sometimes refer to someone as the son of so and so when so and so has several sons, "the, when it is strictly used involves uniqueness." Russell's analysis is:

> 'It is not always false of x that x begat Charles II and that x was executed and that "if x begat Charles II, y is identical with x" is always true of y'.

This analysis can simplified as:

> There exists one and only one x who begat Charles II, and that x was executed.

In either case, the analysis eliminates the definite description or denoting phrase 'the father of Charles II' and thus eliminates the illusion that the phrase in question is a name, the meaning of which is the object to which it refers. In order to fully appreciate the effectiveness of the theory of descriptions we must test its ability to solve the three referring puzzles---the first of which is the puzzle concerning George IV.

If we apply the pattern of analysis provided by the theory of descriptions, our second premise is recognized to be ambiguous because it can be analyzed as either (1) or (2):

(1) One and only one thing wrote Waverly, and George IV
wished to know if that thing was Scott.

(2) George IV wished to know if one and only one thing wrote
Waverly, and if that thing was Scott.

To interpret it as (1) is, according to Russell, to accord to the descriptive phase in question a *primary occurrence*, whereas to interpret it as (2) is to accord to it a *secondary occurrence*. To accord a primary occurrence to a descriptive phrase is to interpret it to have what logicians designate "existential import," which is to regard it as committing one to the existence of its alleged referent. To accord a secondary occurrence to a descriptive phase does not make such commitment.[7]   This distinction will have significant bearing on Russell's resolution to the puzzle concerning the present king of France, but it has no significance here. Either interpretation of premise 2 enables us to appreciate how Russell's theory solves our puzzle regarding George IV. Examination of both interpretations reveals that the troublesome expression 'the author of Waverly' has been *eliminated*, and thus it cannot be substituted for by 'Scott.'

What Russell wants us to understand is that the puzzle only exists because natural languages are misleading. Natural languages deceive us, and it is only through logical analysis that we are able to remove these confusions. What looked like a name 'the father of George IV,' turns out not to be so. The source of confusion lies in the syntax of ordinary language, which treats all substantives the same. They are all treated as designators or names. A proper syntax of the sort provided by Russell's logic distinguishes between true designators and incomplete symbols. In such a logic or "ideal" language, puzzles like the one about George IV could not even arise.

The syntactic rules of ordinary or natural language acknowledges no formal difference between 'Walter Scott was a Scotsman.' and 'The author of Waverly was a Scotsman.' Both are expressions of the subject-predicate format. The rules of syntax for Russell's logic recognize that they are quite different in logical form. While the former is of the genuine subject-predicate form, and says that some predicate applies to the object referred to by the name in question, the latter is a disguised existential assertion which really says:

There exits one and only one x such that x both authored Waverly and is a Scotsman.

The third puzzle, the present king of France puzzle, is solved similarly by applying the theory of descriptions, but here the distinction between a primary and a secondary occurrence of a descriptive phrase becomes all important. According to Russell, the sentence 'The present king of France is bald,' becomes, when analyzed in the manner recommended by the theory of descriptions:

(S) There exists one and only one x such that x is at present king of France and bald.

Its denial, 'The present king of France is not bald,' is, however, ambiguous and subject to the following two analyses depending upon whether or not the descriptive phase 'the present king of France' is accorded a primary or a secondary occurrence. If it is accorded a primary occurrence it becomes:

not (Spo) There exists one and only one x such that x is at present king of France and non-bald.

Since there is at present no king of France to be either bald or non-bald, (S) and not (Spo) are, according to Russell, both false.[8] And although the law of the excluded middle appears to be invalidated, we need not worry. For, according to Russell, when we accord a secondary occurrence to the descriptive phase 'the present king of France' we get:

not (Sso) It is not the case that there exists an x such that x is both at present the king of France and bald.

Interpreted in this way, the denial of 'The present king of France is bald,' is true. According to Russell, this interpretation is the true contradictory of 'The present king of France is bald,' and in this way the law of the excluded middle is preserved, and our paradox is resolved.

The first puzzle, the one concerning negative existential assertions, does not appear to be one which lends itself to solution by means of the theory of descriptions. The sentence in question, 'Apollo does not exist,' does not contain any definite descriptions. Again we are deceived by appearances. According to Russell, what we have here is a paradigm case of how natural languages can deceive us. As far as ordinary language is concerned, the sentence in question is of the subject-predicate format and does not differ in any important respect from 'Finn is a non-philosopher' From the perspective of ordinary language, the subject of predication in this case is my grandson, and the predicate is "is a non-philosopher." Since Finn is only ten months old, the predicate "non-philosopher" can be attributed to him. Similarly, since Apollo, a mythological God, did not actually exist, the predicate "non-existence" can be attributed to him. But, how can a non-existent thing be anything?

The resolution of this puzzle lies in the perfected language of *Principia Mathematica*. This logically perfected language incorporates the Kantian dictum that existence is not a predicate or a property. Like Frege, Russell's analysis treats existence to be a property or attribute of propositional functions. To say that a propositional function exists is to say that it is instantiated. Since a logically proper name is by definition used to name what is momentarily present, it would be redundant to assert that it exists, and to deny its existence is to contradict one's self. Ordinary proper names, which do not refer to what can only be momentarily present, are, according to Russell, really descriptions masquerading as proper names. They are for Russell what Leonard Linsky refers to as *disguised descriptions*.9 We are now in position to understand Russell's solution to the puzzle concerning negative existentials. 'Apollo' is a disguised description. The description which is hidden under the mask of ordinary language, and revealed by consulting a classical dictionary, is according to Russell, 'the sun-god'. Substituting this description for 'Apollo' in (a) produces:

(a) The sun-god does not exist.

This is tantamount to saying that (a) is not about a non-existent entity, but rather is actually a denial that anything instantiates the propositional function 'is a sun-god.' Russell in now in a position to resolve our dilemma concerning the impossibility for (1), (2), and (3) to all be true, by maintaining that although (1) and (3) are true, (2) must be false. (a) is not about Pegasus, but is, instead, about the non-instantiation of the propositional function in question.

Russell's theory of descriptions, which Frank Ramsey praised as "a paradigm of philosophy," stood unchallenged for over thirty years.

This is an astonishing tribute to Russell's ingenuity. Most philosophical theories are under attack within days, if not hours, after their publication. G.E. Moore expressed a serious objection to the idea that existence can only be attributed to propositional functions in 1936. But it was not until 1950 that P. F. Strawson launched his general attack on the theory.

Moore agrees with Frege and Russell that there are uses of 'exists' where the term in question "does not stand for an attribute of an object or individual." While the propositions expressed by 'Some tame tigers growl' and 'Some tame tigers exist' both appear to attribute properties to tame tigers, there is an important difference. The former can be said to assert that there are values of the variable x which instantiate two attributes, namely being tame, and being something which growls. But the latter *cannot* be said to assert that there are values of the variable x which instantiate two attributes: being tame and being existent. Such an assertion would, Moore concedes, be nonsense. Yet he is unwilling to concede that there are no uses of 'exists' where it does stand for an attribute or property of an object.

According to Moore, Russell is wrong in claiming that the attribution of existence to what is referred to by a proper name is meaningless or without sense. Moore reminds the reader that Russell's principle example of a logically proper name is 'this.' Moore then focuses our attention upon the sentence 'This exists.' He argues that in cases where it would be appropriate to say, "This is a tame tiger," it would also be appropriate to point at the object in question and say "This exists," on the grounds that "you can clearly say with truth of any such object, "This might not have existed." Moore cannot understand how it is possible that 'This might not have existed' should be true, unless 'This does in fact exist' is also true, and therefore that the words 'This exists' are significant."10

Strawson claimed in 1950 that Russell's theory of descriptions was still widely accepted among logicians "as giving a correct account of the use of such expressions [definite descriptions] in ordinary language". But, according to Strawson "this theory, so regarded, embodies some fundamental mistakes."11

As I pointed out previously, Russell often uses the words 'sentence' and 'proposition' interchangeably. He also sometimes uses them to mark a difference between a symbolic expression and what it expresses, which is what most philosophers, Frege included, consider a proposition to be. According to Strawson, Russell's fundamental mistake is that he fails to distinguish either sentences or what they express (their meanings) from the *use* of a sentence, on a particular occasion, by a particular person.[12] It is, according to Strawson, only such uses (statements) which can be said to be either true or false. Or, to put it somewhat differently, the predicates "is true" and "is false" can only be attributed to *statements*. They cannot be attributed either to sentences or to their meanings (propositions). To illustrate his objection, Strawson focuses upon the puzzle concerning the present king of France. He asks us to consider the sentence, 'The present king of France is wise,' and to recognize that:

> if one man were to utter it in the reign of Louis XIV and
> another man uttered it in the reign of Louis XV, it would be
> natural to say (to assume) that they were respectively talking
> about different people; and it might be held that the first man,
> in using the sentence, made a true assertion, while the second
> man, using the same sentence, made a false assertion. If on
> the other hand two different men simultaneously... during the
> reign of Louis IV it would be natural to say (assume) that they
> were both talking about the same person, and in that case, in
> using the sentence, they must either both have made a true
> assertion or both have made a false assertion.[13]

In opposition to Russell, Strawson wants us to understand that meaning is a function of sentences like '(a)' and expressions like 'the present king of France,' while referring and truth or falsity are functions of the uses of such sentences or expressions. He claims that the providing the meaning of an expression is to provide "general directions for its use to refer to or to mention particular objects or persons," and that providing the "meaning of a sentence is to give general directions for its use in making true or false assertions." For Strawson, whether or not a sentence or an expression is has a meaning is irrelevant to the question of whether "the sentence, uttered on a particular occasion, is, on that occasion, being used to make a true o false assertion or not, or of whether the expression is, on that occasion, being used to refer to, or mention anything at all."[14]

Strawson argues that Russell's confusion on these matters led him to mistakenly conclude that the relation that holds between the sentence 'The present king of France is wise,' or the proposition it expresses, and the following sentence, or the proposition it expresses, is entailment.

(1) There exists one and only one thing which is at present king of France.

If (1) were entailed by 'The present king of France is wise,' call it S, it would have to follows that when (1) is false, S must also be false. According to Strawson, the relation that actually obtains between S and (1) is presupposition, which he defines as follows. To say that S presupposes (1) is to say that (1) must be true for S to be either true or false. If (1) is false, then S is to be regarded as neither true nor false. Stawson's point can best be appreciated if you ask yourself what would be the right response to make if I were to ask you if the leprechaun in your pocket has on a green hat. The proper response would not be either that he did or that he did not, but rather that the question is inappropriate because there is no leprechaun in your pocket. On Stawson's account, it is mistaken to conclude as did Russell that both S and not (Spo) are false because (1) is false. They are instead, for Strawson, neither true nor false.

A defender of Russell will likely argue that Russell, like most logicians, held that all propositions are either true or false, [15] that this is a matter of definition for Russell, and thus that Strawson who is talking about assertions or statements is guilty or comparing apples to oranges. In *Referring*, L. Linsky illustrates this defense thus:

> Now, of course, no one refutes Euclidean geometry by pointing out that the triangle on the blackboard has an angle sum of more than 1800 when measured with the most accurate instruments. Similarly, we must distinguish between the logical calculus, the propositions which are the values of its variables and the utterances, sayings, or statements which people produce in their everyday use of language. Just as geometry remains unrefuted by measurements of physical triangles, so logic is not refuted by the discovery that there are statements which we would not call either true or false, but (say) exaggerated, or vague, or inaccurate. But this is exactly what Strawson does[16] when he criticizes Russellian logic.[17]

Another way of putting this kind of defense of Russell's theory is to insist, as so many contemporary philosophers do, on the distinction between semantics and pragmatics. Semantics is the study of the truth conditions for sentences, and pragmatics is the study of the actual employment of sentences by particular users in various contexts. Russell can be regarded as a semanticist, Stawson as a pragmaticist. This issue does not end here, however, as not every contemporary philosopher is satisfied with the distinction between semantics and pragmatics, especially in so far as those who live by this distinction tend look down their formalistic noses at what they regard as the plebeian pursuit of the unkempt distinctions of ordinary language.[18]

I will return to this issue when I discuss Wittgenstein's critique at the end of the present chapter. I want now to elaborate some other problems with Stawson's approach, and to point out a distinct advantage of Russell's theory of descriptions over Strawson's presupposition theory. In his *Introduction to Logical Theory*, Strawson extends his notion of presupposition to all four Aristotelian forms. The truth of the existence condition is said by him to be a necessary condition "not of truth simply but of the truth or falsity of such statements."[19] According to Strawson's presupposition theory, if one asserts the following sentence, what he would be asserting is neither true nor false because the subject term denotes a non-existent object.

(E) No Leprechauns are red hat wearers.

But according to both Aristotelian and modern logic, this sentence is by conversion said to be logically equivalent to:

(CE) No red hat wearers are Leprechauns.

Since presupposition condition is satisfied for (CE), green hat wearers do exist, it would seem that stating it would be to state what is either true or false. But how can this be, since the (E) and (CE) would be used to make logically equivalent statements? What Strawson does to avoid this kind of objection is to preface all traditional inferences, conversion, obversion, etc., with the proviso, "Assuming that the statements concerned are either true or false, then." Which is to say that when both sentences are used to make statements having truth values, then relations like conversion, contradiction, etc. can be said to yield those consequences asserted by tradition to be validly inferable. But as Linsky has pointed out, this course of action renders Stawson's view compatible with Russell's. According to Linsky:

> Let us assume that S presupposes S'. What this means is that from the premise that S has a truth-value, it follows that S' is true. But S is true if, and only if, the king of France is wise, and S' is true if, and only if, one, and only one, person is king of France. Therefore the statement that the king of France is wise entails the statement that one, and only one, person is king of France.[20]

Strawson could attempt to sidestep Linsky's objection, and counter my objection concerning the relation of conversion, by insisting that the presupposition condition must be meet for both the subject and the predicate term for the relation of conversion to be valid. But how, Linsky would counter, does that this condition differ from assuming that the statements concerned are either true of false? I, on the other hand, would respond by focusing attention on the following sentence.

No Saturn XXX rockets are being designed by NASA to place a manned United States spacecraft on Uranus.

Suppose someone has misinformed members of the press that NASA has in fact designed a rocket for placing a manned United States spacecraft on Uranus. Suppose further that there are no Saturn XXX rockets, and in fact no rockets of any description are being designed to place such a spacecraft on Uranus. The presupposition condition is not satisfied for either the subject term or the predicate term, and yet it is clear that the displayed sentence could be used to assert a true statement. It is easy to imagine that the director of NASA might well use it in the process of a news conference intended to dispel the rumors in question:

> Gentlemen and ladies of the press I wish to make a statement, and I assure you that what I am about to say is true. Saturn XXX rockets are not being designed to land a manned United States spacecraft on Uranus.[21]

44

What we have is a case where the presupposition condition is not satisfied for either the subject or the predicate term, and we have a paradigm case of what it is to make a statement--a statement which would be, under these imagined circumstances, true. This example prevents Stawson from avoiding the difficulty which the leprechaun case poses for his theory by requiring that both terms meet the presupposition condition. Also, and more importantly, it reveals that there are cases where the presupposition condition is not satisfied for the subject term, and yet one can succeed in making a true statement, or depending on the circumstances, a false one. In addition, it reveals a distinct advantage of Russell's theory over Strawson's.

Russell's analysis of the NASA official's statement would not only capture what the official wishes to state, it also captures the fact that it is true, and avoids the mistaken idea that it is neither true nor false:

> Nothing is both a Saturn XXX rocket, and a rocket being planned to land a United States spacecraft on Uranus.

Previously I discussed Linsky's use of the analogy between formal logic and geometry in rebuttal to Strawson, and I linked this analogy to the distinction between semantics and pragmatics. Although the semantics/pragmatics distinction has achieved venerable status in contemporary philosophy, followers of Wittgenstein do not honor or even respect it. In fact, they argue that this distinction is little more than a ploy used by philosophers to shelter their theories from the kind of critique the later Wittgenstein launched against his own, as well as Russell's, earlier endeavors.

Like Russell, the Wittgenstein of the *Tractatus* attempted to solve philosophical problems through the logical analysis of language. The later Wittgenstein regards this approach to be just another misguided effort in a long series of misguided efforts characteristic of traditional philosophy. Traditional philosophy is, according to his *Investigations*, at the core an ill-conceived discipline which can never succeed because the problems it raises, the questions it poses, are pseudo problems and pseudo questions. Philosophers, according to Wittgenstein, participate in a profession in which constant failure is not only accepted but lauded. Philosophers try to justify their joint endeavor by claiming that its lack of success is in truth a testimonial to the immensely difficult nature of its problems. Wittgenstein spurns this excuse. He argues that the problems of philosophy are not really difficult at all. They are insoluble. They cannot, he claims, by their very nature be *solved*, they can only be *dissolved*.

Philosophical puzzles frustrate and challenge us, and although no real progress towards their solution has been made over the centuries, we continue to hope that some genius will find the key. For Wittgenstein such hopes are ill-founded. He does not regard them to be ill-founded because there is *no* hope that solutions to these problems will ever be forthcoming. Instead, he argues that there is *only* hope. Philosophers are like men lost in a vast but circular maze from which there is no exit accept back through the original entrance.

Wittgenstein rejects the idea that natural language deceives us. It is not in need of refinement and replacement by a language like that conceived of by Russell--a so called "ideal" language. Instead it is its misuse by philosophers, which creates pseudo problems, problems which can only be resolved by allowing natural language to work as it is meant to work. The later Wittgenstein provides us with a unique perspective from which to view the kind of philosophical perplexity he and Russell expressed in their earlier joint endeavors. He does not enter into the fray. He does not attempt to provide solutions to philosophical problems. He is not, as some characterize him, either a verificationist, a behaviorist, a nominalist, or an -ist of any sort.

Wittgenstein's later philosophy is meant to be an *expose* of skepticism, realism, nominalism, idealism, cognitivism, and all the other venerated -isms of philosophy. Ultimately, the problems which philosophy attempts to solve, the problems which dictate choosing between unsatisfactory alternatives, realism vs. nominalism, phenomenalism vs. the causal theory, skepticism vs. phenomenalism, behaviorism vs. cognitivism, etc. are, for Wittgenstein, conjurer's tricks, brilliant slights of hand. But few philosophers want to accept that Wittgenstein is right, especially those of us who have been, or remain, faithful to Plato and his companions on the historical journey that is traditional philosophy. We cannot believe our ears. This guy must be out of his mind. When it was first revealed that the world was round, no one could accept it. The commonplace response to this announcement was "That's crazy, you're out of your mind, just open your eyes and look, isn't it obviously flat?" Wittgenstein would counter such disbelief by questioning the question. He would ask "But how would it look if it were round?"

Still, many philosophers remain unconvinced by Wittgenstein.

They claim that the Wittgensteinian perspective has not been proven to be the case, that Wittgenstein does not offer any deductively valid arguments for his conclusions. True, but he does provide grounds sufficient both to establish his own perspective, and to render suspect the perspectives of the opposition. Let me conclude this chapter by illustrating how I perceive Wittgenstein would approach the disagreement between Strawson and Russell. Consider the following assertions:

(a) Some creatures of mythology are Centaurs.

(b) Some creatures of mythology are not Centaurs.

According to Russell, we understand these sentences, and our understanding of them, their propositional content, can be expressed as "There exists at least one x such that it is both a creature of mythology and a centaur" and "There exists at least one x such that it is both a creature of mythology and a non-centaur." And furthermore, according to Russell's theory, both of these sentences express false propositions because creatures of mythology do not exist. Strawson would agree that there are no creatures of mythology, but his presupposition theory would dictate that neither assertion is true nor false.

Common usage is, however, inconsistent with both of these theories. Both (a) and (b) are, we want to insist, both true. This insistence is based upon our common usage of the expressions 'true' and 'false'. Wittgenstein would remind us of this fact concerning common usage. Simply put, what he would be saying is that we can and do make true and false statements about non existent objects, and none of us are apt to be confused, and think that when we do so, we are committed to the existence of such entities.

I will return to Wittgenstein's critique of traditional philosophy, and specifically his critique of its efforts to provide a theory of knowledge at the end of the next chapter. The next chapter concerns Russell's theory of knowledge, which is in the traditional mold, and as such, vulnerable to Wittgenstein's objections.

Endnotes

1 Russell's statement of the puzzles suffers somewhat by his lack of precision regarding the concepts "sentence," "proposition," and

"statement." In my statement of the puzzles, I endeavor to use the proper word for the entity in question. Our focus here should be upon a sentence, not a proposition nor a statement, the former being simply the standard meaning of a given sentence, and the latter being the use of a particular sentence on a particular occasion by a particular speaker. For a detailed discussion of these concepts, see Odell (1984) pp. 221-227.

2 Russell talks about true propositions, but as Strawson has demonstrated in "On Referring," truth is properly a predicate of statements, not propositions. To be precise (1) should be read as "Sentence (a), when used with its standard meaning, makes a true statement".

3 In defense of this notion one might argue that when we reveal to children that Santa Claus is a mythical personage we are as likely to assert, substituting 'Santa Claus' for 'Pegasus', (a) as (b).

4 Which is to say that they express the same proposition, but to put the matter properly what should be said is that they are both commonly used to make the same statement.

5 Russell (1905) pp. 187-189.

6 Russell (1910) p. 66.

7 Russell (1905) p. 190.

8 What he should have said is that if these two sentences were used with their standard meanings to make statements, both statements would have to be false.

9 Linsky (1967) p. 59.

10 Moore (1936) p. 124.

11 Strawson (1950) p. 163.

12 This is a statement making or asserting use, as contrasted with other conventional uses, for example, warning, promising, postulating, explaining, judging, etc., what Austin refers to as "illocutions." (1962) pp. 98- 163.

13 Strawson (1950) p. 169.

14 Ibid., p. 171.

15 Paradoxically, however, Russell maintains in "The Philosophy of Logical Atomism" that propositions are unreal. Sentence types would have then to serve as the bearers of truth and falsity-- a view very difficult, if not impossible, to maintain.

16 Linsky (19670 P. 91.

17 Although Linsky defends Russell against Strawson on this score, he does side with Stawson in claiming that in ordinary discourse we speak in statements and not propositions. (p. 99).

18 See Baker and Hacker (1984) for an extended attack on this distinction.

19 Strawson (1952) p. 176.

20 Linsky, (1967) p. 94.

21 What he actually says can be translated into a sentence in the E form.

22 See Wittgenstein (1958) Sections 436, p. 129e, and 109, p. 47e.

IV
The Scope and Limits of Knowledge

In this chapter I will explicate Russell's views regarding the nature of human knowledge. Like Hume, Russell is both an empiricist, and an epistemological skeptic. I will also examine G. E. Moore's criticism of Russell's skepticism. I do so because the issue regarding skepticism's validity can best be appreciated and understood by contrasting Russell's views with those of Moore. I will defend Russell's skepticism against Moore's objections, but I will criticize it on other grounds. I will conclude this chapter with a brief sketch of the Wittgensteinian perspective on skepticism.

Russell's views on the subject of human knowledge are stated in a variety of works, including *The Problems of Philosophy*, *Our Knowledge of the External World*, and *An Inquiry into Meaning and Truth* and *Human Knowledge: Its Scope and Limits*. And although Moore has expressed his objections to Russell's form of skepticism in a variety of works on the subject, he nowhere succeeds as well as he does in "Four Forms of Skepticism." In this work, he manages to expresses precisely and clearly both what *philosophical skepticism* is, and what has to be established in order for it to succeed. For these reasons I will restrict my analysis of Moore's critique of Russell's skepticism to it.

Russell's methodological approach is inspired by Descartes, a fact which Russell frequently acknowledges.[1]   Throughout his epistemological works, we find Russell subjecting various kinds of human belief to Cartesian or methodological doubt in an effort to see if any are justified. And while he did as a young philosopher embrace other aspects of *rationalism*, a doctrine associated with Descartes, the theory of knowledge he promotes in the previously mentioned works is essentially *empiricism*. What primarily separates these two schools of philosophy is their respective views regarding the origins of human knowledge. The rationalists hold that much of our knowledge is innate. The empiricists deny this. They hold that all knowledge originates in experience. This debate has a very long history in philosophy, and it continues today. Quine and those who follow him are empiricists. Chomsky and his followers are rationalists. Chomsky's followers, one of whom is Jerry Fodor, dominate "cognitive science," the recently emergent interdisciplinary study consisting of philosophers, psychologists, linguists and computer scientists.

Russell, like empiricism's founder, John Locke, starts with the givens of sense perception, and attempts to infer from them the external world. Russell uses the term 'sense-data' to refer to the sensory givens. For Russell, sense data are the building blocks from which all other empirical beliefs are constructed. Like Locke, Russell is a causal theorist who believes that the data of the senses are caused by physical objects. We experience sense-data and infer from them the existence of physical objects. But like David Hume, empiricism's most inventive advocate, Russell is led to conclude that such inferences are invariably invalid. He is eventually forced to adopt epistemological skepticism, and to assert that while physical objects, other persons, etc. may very well exist, we can never really know that they do.

Russell's application of the Cartesian methodology is not, however, an effort to determine which among our various kinds of belief are certain, but rather to determine which are certain in the highest degree. He says that certainty "may be more or less present, in gradations ranging from absolute certainty down to an almost imperceptible faintness."[2]   But what exactly, one may ask, does Russell mean by 'certain'? Elsewhere[3], he distinguishes between three kinds of certainty, logical, psychological, and epistemological. He explicates the first kind by asserting that "a propositional function is certain with respect to another when the class of terms satisfying the second is part of the class of terms satisfying the first. For example, "x is an animal" is certain in relation to "x is a rational animal." The second kind is the kind of certainty one attaches to a proposition "when he feels no doubt whatever of its truth." The third, and most important kind of certainty occurs when a proposition "has the highest degree of credibility either intrinsically or as the result of an argument." He exemplifies the concept of "degrees of credibility" in terms of addition. Every time he adds up his accounts with the same result he becomes more certain of it. "This increase of conviction goes with an increase of evidence, and is therefore rational."[4] Since credibility amounts to evidential support we can formulate Russell's notion of epistemological certainty as:

> (EC) A belief is epistemologically certain when it has the highest degree of evidential support.

This statement is ambiguous--we can understand the phrase 'highest degree of evidential support' in either a quantitative, or qualitative sense. Russell's example favors the former sense in that the *more often* one adds up his accounts, the greater is the certainty which accrues.

In *Our Knowledge of the External World*, Russell is led to accept as "hard data" only "those beliefs that resist the solvent influence of critical reflection," namely, "the "particular facts of sense" and the "general laws of logic." But instead of requiring the highest degree of evidential support, his criterion is that "there could not be any evidence or reasons, of a non-paththological variety, for doubting them."[5] In short, "hard data" beliefs are regarded as "intrinsically credible beliefs," to use a description he uses elsewhere.[6] (EC) must be amended to reflect this fact.

> (EC') A belief is epistemologically certain when it either is intrinsically credible, or it has the highest degree of evidential support.

A problem remains, however, as regards intrinsic credibility. If we take the claim that a belief is intrinsically credible to mean that "there could not be any evidence to the contrary," we would be forced to accept all sorts of preposterous beliefs as certain. Suppose that someone believes that there is in this room an invisible and intangible monster. Since it would be impossible for there to be any evidence to the contrary, this belief would have to be said to be intrinsically certain! This defect in our definition can be removed by claiming that no belief can be accepted as certain for which there could not be any evidence for or against. This would mean that no belief could qualify as intrinsically certain unless, in addition to its being impossible for there to be any evidence to the contrary, there is evidence or reason in favor of it. In the case of logical principles, the reason in favor of their acceptability would simply be the one favored by Descartes, that their denials are contradictions. In the case of sense-data beliefs, the operative clause would be their undeniable reality. He says, "the immediate facts perceived by sight or touch or hearing do not need to be proved by argument, but are completely self-evident."[7] We can now revise (EC') to reflect these considerations as:

(EC'') A belief is epistemologically certain when (a) its denial is a contradiction, (b) its content is restricted to presently existing sense-data, or (c) it has the highest degree of evidential support.

In *The Problems of Knowledge*, Russell distinguishes between *knowledge of truths*, and *knowledge of objects*.[8] He then proceeds to focus upon the latter kind of knowledge and to distinguish under that heading two separate kinds, namely, *knowledge by acquaintance*, and *knowledge by description*, which he accomplishes in the following passages:

...in the presence of my table I am acquainted with the sense-data that make up the appearance of my table--its color, shape, hardness, smoothness, etc.... My knowledge of the table as a physical object, on the contrary, is not direct knowledge.... my knowledge of the table is the kind which we shall call 'knowledge by description'.[9]

In *Our Knowledge of the External World*, Russell marks the same distinction by distinguishing between knowledge which is *derivative* and knowledge which is *primitive*.

Guided by conceptions inherent in his distinction between knowledge by acquaintance and knowledge by description, especially when understood as a distinction between primitives and derivations,

Russell is forced to adopt Humian skepticism. [10] In other words, it matters not how numerous are my sense impressions supporting the idea that there is a table in front of me, its independent existence cannot be deduced from that support. Physically existing objects are conceived of as objects which will continue to exist when no one is around to sense them. Nothing presently existent can be the basis for inferring the existence of what is not present.

It is important to realize that just how different *philosophical* skepticism is from ordinary or everyday skepticism. All of us are skeptical on occasion. Philosophical skepticism, unlike the everyday kind, is non-contextually relevant. It does not fluctuate. Changing agents, locations, times, or circumstances are irrelevant. Today I am skeptical as regards whether an unreliable acquaintance will keep an appointment to serve as a crew member for an afternoon of sailing. Last week we had a similar arrangement, but then I was not the slightest bit skeptical about his showing up. And the reason I was not skeptical then was because I knew that he was in the company of a conscientious third member of our sailing crew. To be philosophically skeptical about this kind of occurrence is, however, tantamount to the conviction that no person what-so-ever could ever know that any other individual will keep an appointment. The concept of philosophical skepticism (PS) can best be expressed as any instantiation of Ψ in the following principle:

PS: No human could ever know anything about the existence or characteristics of anything of kind Ψ.

To adopt Humian skepticism (classical philosophical skepticism) is to argue for the instantiation of the Ψ in PS for all of the following objects of knowledge: Gods; the past; the future; the self; and other persons. Or to put the matter somewhat differently, no human could ever know with certainty anything other than analytic propositions (their denials are contradictions) and propositions descriptive of the immediate givens of sense. Or to cast the matter in terms of doubt and belief, it is always possible to doubt the truth of any belief except those the denials of which are contradictions, and those which simply describe present momentary sensory fields.

Russell's arguments in favor of doubt regarding the existence of physical objects, other persons, the past, and the self are of four kinds: first, there is what I shall refer to as "the differing persons and perspectives argument;" second, the argument based upon illusions or hallucinations; third, the dream argument; and forth, the malevolent deity argument. The differing persons and perspectives argument concludes that we can never know for certain that any given physical object exists because there will always be evidence both for and against its having any given characteristic. [11] The same physical object can appear to the *same* person at different times to have contradictory properties. The same physical object can appear to *different* people, at the same or different times to have contradictory properties. My shirt looks white to me now, but in a discotheque under strobe-lighting it will appear luminous blue. So what difference does that make? According to Russell, it makes a big difference as "there is no reason for regarding some of these as more really its colour than others." From which it follows that I can never be certain what the real color of my shirt is. And, moreover, that I can never be certain of any other property of it, or of any property of any object. Since Russell assumes that these considerations also justify doubt regarding any object's existence, he must think that we cannot know that any given physical object exists unless we can determine at least one of its properties.

The argument from illusion, which lumps together illusions and hallucinations, provides further reason for claiming that one can never know that a physical object exists or has the properties it appears to have. A stick appears bent when immersed in water, and, like Macbeth, we are all capable of seeing a dagger before us when one is not there to be seen.

The dream argument, Descartes favorite ploy, turns on the fact that some of our dreams involve content realistic enough to be indistinguishable from the content of daily experiences. We dream that we are being chased by a vicious dog, and we wake up terrified. The dream elicited the same response as would have occurred if a vicious dog had actually been at our heels. Since it is always *possible that* one is presently dreaming, how can one ever be certain that what one is experiencing is really happening?

Russell thinks that the world could have been created by a malevolent deity. He claims that no evidence exists which would establish with certainty that the universe was not created by such an entity. But if this is a possibility, then it is *possible that* this deity created the universe just a second ago and my memories of the past regarding the existence of it and its contents are all simply the figments of my faulty memory bank--one he has created with the express purpose of deceiving me.

Russell's views on this subject can be summarized in the form of an argument as follows:

> (1) It is always *possible that* one is mistaken when one judges that a given physically existent thing, other person, or even one's own self exists, has existed, or has the properties one takes it to have because of the possibility of conflicting evidence based upon differing persons and perspective, or the possibility that one is hallucinating, having an illusory experience, dreaming, or being deceived.

In addition, he correctly assumes that:

> (2) If it is certain that p, then it is not possible that not p.

From which it follows that:

> (3) If it is possible that not p, then it is not certain that p.

Which when generalized becomes:

> (3') If it is always possible that not p, then it is never certain that p.

He also alleges that (4) and apparently presupposes that (5):

> (4) Beliefs about the future and about Gods are, even from the perspective of most non-philosophers, never certain.

> (5) All of our beliefs either concern or can be reduced to beliefs about: physical objects; other persons; the past; the future; the self; God or Gods; and sense data, or they are analytic.

From (1), (2), (3'), (4), and (5), it follows that:

> (C) Unless p is a tautology or a belief about sense-data, p can never be known with certainty to be true.

G. E. Moore in his, "Four Forms of Skepticism," criticizes Russell for failing to distinguish between two senses of 'possible,' namely, 'possible for,' and 'possible that.' The relevance of this distinction pertains to premise (1) of Russell's argument. Moore claims that Russell fails to use the appropriate sense of 'possible' in premise (1), and because of this, Russell's conclusion cannot be validly inferred from his premises. Although Moore does not use the term 'equivocation' to characterize Russell's mistake, he is, nevertheless, accusing Russell of having committed the *fallacy of equivocation.*

Suppose that you are a death row prisoner and I am your lawyer. I have just returned from trying to persuade the Governor to commute your death sentence, and I am informing you regarding that decision. You immediately ask me if he is going to commute your sentence. Suppose I answer your question with, "It's possible." What I have said is ambiguous. It can mean that it is *possible that* he will do so, which means that I have good, though not conclusive, grounds for thinking that he will. But it can also mean that it is *possible for* him to do so, which only means that he has the authority to do so. While it is *possible for* any governor to commute any prisoner's sentence, it may not be *possible that* a particular governor will commute a particular prisoner's sentence. For it to be possible that he will do so, there must be evidence that he will do so. Suppose that the Governor had heatedly reminded me that he very much favored the death penalty, and revealed to me both that he believed you were "guilty as hell," and that he was absolutely unwilling to commute your sentence. Under these circumstances, it would be false for me to tell you that it is possible that the Governor will commute your sentence, even though it remains within his power to do so. Given that I am squeamish and want to avoid your predictably unhappy reaction to this news, I might purposely leave out the details of my meeting with the Governor in the hope that you will "grasp at straws," and interpret my "It's possible," as "possible that he will." Were I to do this, I would be committing the fallacy of equivocation. I could defend what I have said on the grounds that since it is in his power to do so, my premise was true. Yet, what I expect you to conclude is that there is a chance that you will not be executed--a conclusion which requires the premise, "It's possible" to be interpreted in the sense in which it would be false. What I want you to do is interpret "Its Possible" as "It is possible that the governor will commute your sentence."

Moore employs this distinction to refute Russell. What

57

Moore wants us to conclude is that premise (1) in Russell's argument in favor of skepticism is false. It only appears to Russell to be true because he is equivocating on the possibility of dreaming, hallucinating, etc. From the fact that we dream realistically, and are, in addition, subject to illusions, hallucinations, and viewing things differently from differing perspectives, it does not follow that it is always possible that one is mistaken regarding the existence or properties of a given physical object. Instead, what does follow is that it is always possible for one to be mistaken as regards the existence or properties of any object.[12]

Would it be possible to save Russell's argument for skepticism by substituting 'possible for' for 'possible that' in premise (1) ? No! That would make premise (1) true, but then (C) would not follow.

According to Moore, the skeptic must establish that whenever, for example, one claims to be certain that he is seeing a table or any other physical object, there is always *concrete* evidence that he is dreaming, etc. But all that the skeptic is justified in asserting is, according to Moore, that it is possible for the subject of such experiences to hallucinate, dream, etc. Moore's analysis of skepticism in terms of the distinction between "possible that" and "possible for" enables one to understand what must be accomplished if we are going to take skepticism seriously. I remain unconvinced, however, that Moore is right and that Russell is mistaken. I do not think that "possible that p" is always an *inappropriate* description of those cases where there is no concrete evidence that p. Suppose we have two women who have just parked their car in front of their local bank with the intention of withdrawing money. As they leave the car to go into the bank someone runs out of the bank with a bag of money in one hand and a revolver in the other. The bank manager is in pursuit and yells, "Stop him, he just robbed the bank." The women register both shock and recognition regarding the robber. One of them asks the robber, "John what in the world is going on?" He shoves her aside, and jumps into a car driven by an accomplice. They speed away. When the women are interrogated, and shown what the bank's cameras have recorded, they break down and reveal that the robber is the son of one of them, and the husband of the other. The police apprehend John at home. When confronted with the evidence against him, he continues to protest his innocence, although he has no alibi. He was at home alone all day and was not seen by anyone. His prospects are slim indeed!

But at this point Sherlock Holmes appears at the police station and claims, as he characteristically does, that the police are mistaken. He claims that it may not have been John who robbed the bank. "Do you have any concrete evidence that he did not rob the bank, was he seen somewhere else at the time the bank was robbed, was he at work?" asks the Inspector Lestrade. Holmes replies that he does not have any evidence to disprove John robbed the bank, but that there are facts which must not be discounted. Years ago, when he was pursuing his arch enemy Professor Moriarty through the streets of London, Moriaty escaped near St James Hospital. The next day Holmes read in the Times that someone had kidnapped a male child from that very same hospital, and that this child was a member of a set of identical male twins. The child was never recovered. Holmes reminds Inspector Lestrade that Moriarty has always boasted that he will commit the perfect crime. Holmes then argues that if Moriaty was responsible for the kidnapping, the scenario of this crime is consistent with the hypothesis that it was Moriarty's attempt to commit the perfect crime. Moriarty could have raised the boy to be a criminal, kept close watch on John and his family, knew that the women of the house always did their banking on Tuesdays, and knew that John never left the house on that day. On the basis of these considerations, Holmes concludes that it is possible that John did not commit the robbery.

What this case shows is that "possible that not p" does not require there to be concrete evidence that p is not the case. Instead, all that is required is that one provide *good reasons* or be able to provide a plausible case that not p. Like Holmes, the skeptic offers a "fact-based scenario" which would, in spite of any concrete evidence favoring p, establish that not p remains a factual possibility. This is precisely what the skeptic does when he points out that as a matter of fact humans do hallucinate and dream, and are often deceived by their senses.

The role of the malevolent deity is, however, harder to validate. It certainly is not factually based. Moore treats the argument based upon the possible existence of such an entity separately. He doesn't attack it as just another example of the failure to distinguish "possible that" from "possible for." He would agree that, unlike dreaming hallucinating etc., the possibility of a malevolent deity has no factual basis. According to Moore, the hypothesis of the malevolent deity is simply a logical possibility--its denial is not a contradiction. Moore claims that what Russell seems to be asserting on the grounds of the logical possibility of the malevolent deity is that nothing which one experiences regarding, for example, my computer's existence, that I see it, feel it, hear it, etc. is logically inconsistent with its not actually existing. Moore grants that this is true, but argues that it would be less rational to believe all the propositions one has to accept in order to accept Russell's argument, than for one to believe that one knows that the computer on which one appears to write does actually exist. But then he confesses that he has no criterion upon which to base a decision regarding which among these various propositions it is most rational to believe.[13]

Unlike Moore, I think we can establish that it is more rational for me to be certain that the computer on which I now write does exist, than to be convinced by any of Russell's arguments for skepticism, including the one based upon the possibility that a malevolent deity exists. Even if I am right, and Moore is wrong, in thinking that the Skeptic's principle argument is not an example of the equivocation fallacy, an independent argument can be constructed to show that Russell's brand of philosophical skepticism must be mistaken.

I remind the reader that according to Russell, we can never be certain of the truth of any belief other than those whose denials are contradictions (tautologies) and those which describe only a object presently existing in a sensory field (beliefs about sense-data). Beliefs about Gods, physical objects, other persons, the self, the past and the future, are all subject to doubt. Russell has provided arguments to establish that all beliefs about these various kinds of thing can be doubted. There is, however, one class of beliefs which he has nowhere considered. To say that the word 'dog' means or refers to a domesticated carnivorous mammal originally derived from several wild species is to provide a definition. Definitions are not analytical--their denials are not contradictions. Nor do they describe sense-data. Since they are neither of these kinds of belief, we must, if we accept Russell's account of this matter, assign them to the realm of the doubtful. But if they are so regarded, how can anyone be certain about anything which he claims? Any belief claim is, of necessity, expressed in language, and language use presupposes the truth of indefinitely many definitions. Since all of the skeptic's arguments consist in various claims, it follows that all of his arguments are themselves doubtful. Why then, should anyone take them seriously? Perhaps it is this kind of insight which motivated Wittgenstein to respond to the skeptic's concern regarding such questions as "How do you know that this is a dog?" with the philosophically perplexing answer, "I know English!" This interpretation is at the very least consistent with Wittgenstein's assessment of the philosophical enterprise.

As I pointed out previously, Wittgenstein's later work attempts to establish the unpopular thesis that philosophical questions cannot be solved, they can only be dissolved, and their dissolution can only occur if we recognize them for what they are. Let us now consider how Wittgenstein would, for example, dissolve philosophical skepticism regarding knowledge of other minds.

For Wittgenstein, knowledge of other minds is by definition grounded in behavior. We "misspeak" when we talk about knowledge of other minds as somehow insufficient, when we adopt skepticism, or alternately behaviorism. All we are justified in concluding is that we cannot be aware of the contents of another person's consciousness. According to Wittgenstein, the confusion originates with the philosopher's assumption that we *do* have knowledge of our own consciousness. But this can mean nothing other than that we are aware of it, or are self-conscious. We cannot help being aware of our own consciousness. 'Knowledge' and 'understanding' are, however, terms of accomplishment. What accomplishment is there to being what one cannot help being? If 'knowledge' and 'understanding' can be said to refer to anything, then what they refer to is not some inner process, but rather some episode involving a person, his actions, and a context of occurrence. Wittgenstein maintains that claiming to know, for example, that one's self is in pain is a kind of grammatical nonsense, which only seems to pass muster because it *does* make sense to talk about knowing that another person is in pain. This confusion leads to further confusion. The fact that we cannot be mistaken about our own case is taken by most empiricists, including Russell, to be a basis for claiming that such "awareness"--shift to "knowledge"-- is never present in the second person case. Having now inadvertently *redefined* knowledge as a kind of first person awareness, these philosophers are led to embrace skepticism regarding other minds. We are never *aware* of another person's consciousness, so we can never *know* that they are conscious.

Many philosophers today are not convinced by Wittgenstein's dissolution to the problem under consideration. They claim, among other things, that H. P. Grice's distinction between meaning and *conversational implicature* can be used to defend Russell against Wittgenstein. Following Grice, they claim that although one would never use the epistemic[14] sense of 'know' to say that one knows that one's self is in pain, it would not be false to do so. According to Grice, specifiable conventional principles govern our communication with one another, principles like, "Do not say what is obvious or superfluous." On this view, the reason we do not say about ourselves that we know we are in pain is that to do so would be to say what is obvious to us all.[15]

Hacker (1996) argues that Wittgenstein would not agree that the principle of redundancy is operative, or presupposed in such cases. He would not agree that failure to satisfy it would render the statement either false or truth-valueless. Hacker argues that Wittgenstein would recognize as meaningful the non-epistemic use of 'know' in "I know I am in pain." when it is used for emphasis. It would amount to or convey the same idea as "I am in pain." But according to Hacker, as a knowledge claim, Wittgenstein would regard it as nonsense. Moreover, if Grice's view were correct, then "I don't know whether I am in pain" would ordinarily have to be false. Its being ordinarily false is what accounts for its being pointless to say "I know I am in pain." But for Wittgenstein it is not ordinarily false, it is just nonsense.[16]

Endnotes

[1] Russell (1912) p. 18; (1929) p. 61; (1940) p. 124.

[2] Ibid., (1912) p. 117.

[3] Russell (1948) p. 396.

[4] Ibid., (1948) p. 342.

[5] Russell, (1929) p. 60.

[6] Russell (1948) p. 395.

[7] Russell (1929) p. 58.

[8] Russell (1912) p. 44.

[9] Ibid., pp. 46-47.

[10] Russell (1912) pp. 7-11.

[11] Moore (1959) pp. 219-222.

[12] Ibid., p. 226.

[13] As opposed to 'know' being used for emphasis.

[14] Grice (1967) pp. 65-68.

[15] Hacker (1996) pp. 245-247.

V
The Mind-Body Problem

The mind-body problem has been around for a long time. But Descartes is the philosopher most responsible for the considerable importance which it has received in modern philosophy. It was Descartes who insisted that there is an *essential* difference between mind and body, and by so doing generated concern regarding how is it possible for them to interact. I feel confident that when I decide to raise my arm that, with bodily effort, I can raise it as high as I desire. But if my mind and body are completely different substances, as Descartes insists, how can an occurrence within a mental substance, my conscious desire to raise my arm, cause a material substance, my arm, to go up? Descartes himself offered a solution to this problem--one which has been the subject of much ridicule. Few professors of philosophy can resist humorous treatment of it in introductory courses. His solution was that the interaction between mind and body takes place in the pineal gland. What possible help is this idea his critics ask scornfully. The pineal gland is no more nor less material than any other body part, including one's arm.

For nearly three hundred and fifty years philosophers have tried to solve this problem. Descartes followers scrapped the unfortunate hypothesis that it was in the pineal gland that the interaction between these two utterly distinct substances took place. They provided solutions of their own, which were, though not ridiculous, most assuredly quaint. Malebranche and Geulincx posited the theory known as *occasionalism.* This solution claims that God created both a material world and a mental world, and set them both in motion in such ways that a mental action, a thought, is always paralleled by the appropriate material action, in the case of our example, the raising of my arm. Mind and body are said to be like two separate clocks set up to keep perfect time with one another. When clock A's hands indicate the hour, say three o'clock, clock B chimes three times. It appears that when clock A's hands are at a given position this causes clock B to chime appropriately. Like Descartes himself, his followers were *dualists*—those philosophers who believe that there are just two basic substances in the universe. Another way to resolve the mind /body problem is to adopt a *monistic* approach. Monists believe that there is just one basic substance in the universe.

Monism comes in two primary flavors--*materialism* and *idealism*. Idealists hold that everything is really mind or spirit. Material things are simply modes, or ways of being mental. Material substance is, according to the idealist, simply an illusion. Berkeley and Hegel are idealists. Materialists hold that everything is really matter. For them, consciousness is simply a manifestation or mode of matter. Contemporary scientific materialists, of whom there are too many to mention, hold that consciousness is simply a brain state. Materialism and idealism are both reductionistic in character. One reduces everything in the universe to mind or spirit, and the other reduces everything in the universe to matter.

Materialism has also spawned what is known as behaviorism, of which there are at least two varieties. There are those who maintain the radical or strict form of behaviorism, which is the view that consciousness is an illusion, that the only existent things are bodies and their behavior or actions. They explain all so-called "psychological states," for example, wishing, believing, knowing, disliking, etc., in behavioristic terms. A person who dislikes another person will ignore, find fault with, disagree with, and avoid that other person.

A second and more sophisticated or criteriological form of behaviorism, sometimes referred to as "soft behaviorism," and sometimes as "methodological behaviorism," maintains that the only *criteria* for whether or not one knows something, merely believes that something, or feels hatred, pain, sadness, etc., are behavioral criteria. According to this form of behaviorism, when a person sustains a severe injury, and that person moans, groans, and whimpers, then that person is almost certainly in pain.

The first variety of behaviorism is easy to refute. One way to do so is to call attention to Wittgenstein's pithy reminder that "pain behavior, and pain behavior accompanied by pain, what greater difference could there be?" The second or criteriological variety is actually irrelevant to the mind/body problem. It is an epistemological and not a metaphysical view. It is only pertinent to the issue of how it is that we *know* when another person is in pain.

Present day materialists argue against all forms of behaviorism, by arguing that any account of human behavior has to recognize its inner causes. They argue that these inner *causes* are neurophysiological states or *functions*.

Hillary Putnam is credited with taking the idea that brain states are functions, and developing it into a full blown philosophical doctrine known as *functionalism*. He argues that there is a serious problem with scientific materialism. What, he asks, and I embellish, would we conclude regarding a being from another planet who although he acts and talks just as we do, turns out not to have a brain, but has instead a functioning silicon-like organ, which seems to cause him behave in conscious fashion? Would we conclude that he was not conscious? We might, but according to Putnam, we would not be entitled to do so. Everything he does suggests that he is every bit as conscious as we are. We should instead, says Putnam, recognize that his organ like our brain serves the same function.

This idea that brain states are functional states is an idea which has become ensconced within cognitive science. Cognitive scientists, following the lead of Jerry Fodor, the instigator if not inventor of cognitive science, adopted the functionalistic approach, and argued that what we think of as consciousness is like a computer's program. Conscious states, like thinking, wishing, fearing, etc., become, on this account of the matter, just different brain functions. Eventually talk about functions gets refined, if not rejected, in favor of talk about computations. The brain is said to contain within itself, at inception, computationalistic programs. And these programs are said to be responsible for all our behavior including language use. In fact, according to Fodor, this innate program is itself a full blown language, complete with all the rules needed to generate all past, present, and future natural languages. Fodor claims that his view is consistent with what is commonly referred to as "folk psychology." Folk psychology, for its defenders, is the view that human behavior is best explained as a causal consequence of certain internal states, namely, beliefs, emotions, intentions, etc. The reason it is called folk psychology is that its defenders claim that this is the way ordinary non-philosophers explain human behavior.

Even more recently, another approach to this problem has taken shape in the work of materialists like Paul Churchland. According to Churchland, the natural languages which ordinary people use to describe psychological facts, and the concepts incorporated within these languages--folk psychology--consists simply in learned responses. As such they are no more valid than any other learned responses, for example, the ancient and medieval view that the earth is flat. According to this kind of account, since our folk psychology could turn out to be as false as have so many other commonly held beliefs, it is possible that a better form of psychology or theory could be constructed, one which would not recognize the existence of mental states (beliefs, thoughts, etc.) but would instead *eliminate* them.[1]

This view, known as "eliminative materialism," solves the traditional problem by eliminating the "problem causing language," just as Russell's theory of descriptions eliminated the problem causing language of referring. Not only am I sure that Russell would have approved of this procedure, there is textual evidence to support the contention that he flirted with the underlying assumptions of eliminative materialism long before the position became defined or recognized. I say "flirted with" because, after a brief courtship, he abandons it.

Russell discussed this topic many times during his lifetime, but to my mind some of his most interesting and original ideas regarding it are contained in a fairly obscure article entitled, "Mind and Matter in Modern Science."[2] It is this essay which supports my contention that Russell's stance on the mind/body problem has relevance to the current debate between eliminative and non-eliminative materialists.

Russell begins his discussion of the mind-body problem by substituting the word 'physicalism' for the word 'materialism,' and then defines 'physicalism' as the view that all events are subject to the laws of physics.[3] Then he points out that there is no reason to believe that matter exists if by matter one means something extended in space, hard, resistant and impenetrable. Which is to say, in opposition to Descartes, that there is no such thing as material substance. A physical object is not, according to Russell, a material substance or a persistent thing. Instead, physical things are collections of brief events, which are "ordered in the four dimensional manifold of space-time". He also accepts the view of physics that energy exists, and that its total amount is constant although its distribution constantly changes.[4]

As regards Descartes' mental substance, Russell again takes the view of "modern physics". For Descartes, the word 'I' refers to a thinking substance. For Russell, the word 'I' is a simply a term of grammar, and, as far as he is concerned, all that we really know about thoughts can be expressed without using the word in question. According to Russell, personal identity is not identical with some persistent and specific mental substance, but rather it is a specific kind of causal connection, namely memory, between a series of events.[5] In this way he *eliminates* talk of the self and its reputed attributes in favor of a scientifically refined theory, and is therefore at this point leaning strongly in the direction of eliminative materialism.

He proceeds by asking if there are any characteristics by which some of the events of the world can be classified as mental and some as physical, and if they can, do the two kinds of events overlap. He answers these questions by first of all defining precisely what he means by physical events and what he means by mental events. Physical events are defined as those events which are the domain of physics. Mental events are defined as those events which we perceive. He then points out that the although the relation between these two kinds of events is complicated, mental events must, precede physical ones in that mix called knowledge. It is only because we perceive tables or chairs that we can ask about their ultimate composition or nature.[6]

Since Russell's view is that one event may really be a group of events occurring in a restricted "spatio-temporal region," it follows that "a bit of brain matter" may be only a group of events, and so one's thoughts, feelings, etc., may only be constituents of this group. From which he concludes that the only difference between the mental and the physical is a matter of "logical level." As the university is a concept at a different level of generality than the concept of each of its buildings, playing fields, offices, etc., the concept of the brain is likewise related to the concept of each of its thoughts, feelings, etc.[7]

Russell concludes this essay by summarizing for us his position concerning the traditional mind and body problem. He reminds us that the traditional issue depended upon distinguishing between material and mental substances. And that since he rejects these notions, his account can be neither that of the idealist nor the materialist. But we cannot, he contends, and here he parts company with the eliminative materialists, reject the existence of mental events since on his account the physical is *inferred from* the mental. We must, according to Russell, perceive events before we can theorize about them.[8]

Russell's objection to the idea that there are no mental events, the view of the eliminative materialist, is that when a philosopher makes such a claim, he is, whether he does or does not recognize it, committed to the view that we would never be able to conceptualize or talk about physical things, that the elimination of the one kind of thing would eliminate the other kind of thing. To borrow from Kant, conception without perception would be empty. Another way of putting Russell's point against eliminative materialism is to imagine asking an eliminative materialist if he really believes that there are no mental events. If he answers that he does, it follows that there is at least one belief in the world, and he is thus contradicting himself. But if he answers that he does not believe it, then why should we?

Russell remains, however, true to the spirit of scientific materialism by claiming that something akin to it might well be true even if it were rash to insist that it is. This something is, he tells us, based on the so-called "supremacy of physics." Russell accepts the implication of quantum theory that the laws of atomic physics cannot be regarded as deterministic, but insists that the physics of large bodies remains deterministic And he concludes, as usual in skeptical fashion, that there is some, although not by any means conclusive, reason for believing that our mental lives are controlled by the laws of physics.[9]

Endnotes

[1] Churchland (1984).

[2] Russell (1946).

[3] Ibid., p. 151.

[4] Ibid., p. 155.

[5] Ibid., p. 156.

[6] Ibid., pp. 160-161.

[7] Ibid., p. 162.

[8] Ibid., p. 162.

[9] Ibid., p. 163.

VI
Ethics

Ethics can be understood as either a technique for attaining a good or meaningful life, or as an analytic discipline which attempts to critically formulate and evaluate ethical codes. The teachings and works of men like Christ, Gautama Buddha, Confucius, and other mystics and holy men, and philosophers like Plato, Epicurus, Epictetus, Spinoza, and Nietzsche, as well as novelists like Tolstoy and Dostoevsky, are all concerned with discovering how to live a proper life. These men were not concerned with questions like: "How is it possible, if possible at all, to justify an ethical code?" "What are the advantages of rule over act utilitarianism?" "How do we actually use terms like 'good', 'right', 'duty', 'wrong', etc.?" These questions are, however, commonly addressed by, and define much of the work of, the professional ethicist. Some ethicists mark the difference between the pursuit of meaningful existence, and the work of the professional ethicist by distinguishing between "practical ethics" and "theoretical ethics."[1] Russell was concerned with both practical and theoretical ethics. His theoretical ethics are primarily those of a utilitarian. His views regarding the meaning of life issue are complicated. He vacillated between being both nihilistic and pessimistic, and being more or less affirmative and hopeful about human existence. In his early years, he sought and found in Spinoza's writings what he thought was the solution to the problem of human existence. He adopted, and continued for several years, to take very seriously Spinoza's view that a meaningful existence was

69

only possible through the intellectual love of God. In this chapter, I shall restrict myself to Russell's theoretical ethics. In the next and last chapter I will address, among other topics, his views regarding meaningful human existence.

As a professional philosopher, Russell was not primarily concerned with ethics. His efforts to develop a theory of ethics are limited to two works, one early in his career, "The Elements of Ethics" (1910), based on, as he acknowledges, G. E. Moore's *Principia Ethica*, and one much later, *Human Society in Ethics and Politics* (1954). In the earlier work he relies heavily on the notion of ethical intuition. In the later work he rejects this idea because it makes ethics far too subjective. His focus in the later work is to find an objective basis for ethics. In both works, he defends consequentialism.

The views Russell expresses in the earlier work are not easy to sort out. He attempts to clarify the concepts of "right" and "wrong" action, and "good" and "bad" consequence. In the very first paragraph of "The Elements of Ethics," Russell disputes the fact/value distinction favored by many ethicists. These ethicists hold that ethics is concerned solely with the dimensions of "good" and "bad," and that science is concerned solely with "truth" and "falsity." Russell contends that "the study of ethics is not something outside science and co-ordinate with it: it is merely one among sciences."[2] In his recent book on Russell's philosophy A. J. Ayer criticizes Russell for holding this view.[3] I disagree with Ayer, and later in the present chapter I will argue that it is one of Russell's most important and interesting insights.

In consequentialistic fashion, Russell defines right conduct in terms of whether or not the consequences of the conduct in question "are likely to be good, or if not wholly good, at least the best possible under the circumstances."[4] Like G. E. Moore in *Principia Ethica*, Russell claims that "good" and "bad" are non-natural properties of actions. For Russell this means that there are no yardsticks for measuring values. When we are uncertain as regards the length and width of a table's top, all we have to do to resolve our dilemma is apply a measuring devise to its surface. But no devises exist which enable us to determine value. Like "redness," "goodness" and "badness" cannot be defined. But unlike "redness," they cannot be seen. For Russell "goodness" and "badness" are simply "qualities which belong to objects independently of our opinions just as much as round and square do." From which it follows, according to Russell, that in any disagreement between two people regarding whether something is good or bad, "only one can be right."[5]

If, however, we adopt the view that good and bad are non-natural properties, and a serious disagreement arises regarding whether or not an action is one or the other, we are, according to Russell, left entirely on our own. We know that both parties cannot be right, but this fact alone cannot, he says, answer either of the following questions, "Are either of the disputants correct?," "If so, which one?". It could be that the action is neither good nor bad, but simply neutral. But even if it is one or the other, we are left with the question of which one it is. Answering this question is not easy, Russell laments, since "it may be very hard to know which is right."[6]

This fact does not prevent us from recognizing that there are two senses of 'good'. There is the 'good' of the sentence 'That is a good thing to do,' which is equivalent in meaning with the sentence 'That is the right thing to do.' There is also the 'good' of 'Pleasure is good.' Here what is meant is equivalent in meaning with what is meant by the sentence 'Pleasure is something which ought to exist on account of its intrinsic value.' It is the latter sense of 'good', which he identifies as referring to a non-natural property, and on which he has directed his attention up to this point in the paper under consideration. He now turns to the former sense of 'good,' and he explicates it by focusing upon the concept of "right conduct."

Philosophers, according to Russell, fall into two different camps as regards what method should be utilized to determine whether an action is right or wrong. Utilitarians claim that the test should be in terms of whether or not its consequences are good or bad. Intuitionists, claim that whether or not an action is right or wrong is to be determined by the approval or disapproval of the moral conscience. Russell believes that we must combine both theories to get a complete account of right and wrong.

Intuitionism maintains that rational intuition is the only means we possess for determining, among the various courses of action open to us, the best course of action. But how are we to determine who is right when our intuitions conflict with one another? We can argue with one another and try our best to persuade the other that he is wrong, but at the end of the day each one of us may remain entirely unconvinced by the other's efforts. Russell attempts to resolve such issues in typical consequentialistic fashion by defining the *objectively best action* as that one, among the various alternative actions open to us, which has the best consequences. He refers to this kind of action as being the *most fortunate* of those available, yet he does not consider the most fortunate act to be objectively the right thing to do. Instead, he defines the objectively right course of action to be the wisest action or that action which, "when account is taken of all the available data, gives us the greatest expectation of good on the balance, or at least the least expectation of evil on balance." Russell's decision to regard the objectively best action in this way is primarily based upon his recognition that there are clear cases where the most fortunate course of action would not be the objectively right thing to do. The objective consequences for society would clearly have been better had the nurses of certain individuals, those who brought about large scale death and destruction, killed them at birth. Yet as Russell recognizes, it would not have been objectively right for those entrusted with their care to have engaged in infanticide, since according to Russell, it would have been highly improbable that any given child would turn out to be a danger to society. We all know how evil Hitler turned out to be, but who could have predicted it at his birth?[7]

No person can foresee the future, or determine the full course of consequences which any action can have. Moreover, since it is impossible for an agent ever to determine what would have been the consequences of the alternatives which were not chosen, these consequences could not be compared with the consequences of the chosen course of action. Hence it is impossible to determine if the chosen action was actually the best of all the alternatives.

These considerations justify Russell's choice of the "wisest course of action" or the action which in the light of all the information the agent possesses will probably have the best result, as what is "right" for the agent to do. In this way he provides a compromise between the purely subjective choice, unacceptable because it makes ethics indefensibly subjective, and the indeterminable objectively best action. Russell does not let the matter rest here. He proceeds by distinguishing what is the objectively best thing to do from the subjectively right thing to do, and by so doing clarifies for us precisely what kind of consequentialism he favors.

In the objective sense of 'ought,' a person ought, according to Russell, to do what is objectively right. Paradoxically, however, he also maintains that in the subjective sense of the word in question a person can be obligated to do what is objectively wrong. It is at this point that Russell's ethical theory takes an interesting twist. He now identifies morality with the subjectively right thing to do. He claims that agents are to be *praised* or *blamed* depending upon whether or not they act to bring about what they would judge to be right after an "appropriate amount of candid thought." The appropriate amount of candid thought is, for Russell, a function of the "difficulty and the importance of the decision."[8]

The upshot of these considerations is that for Russell there are at least three varieties of consequentialism: (1) the kind that judges the rightness of an action in terms of the most fortunate consequences; (2) the kind that judges the rightness of an action in terms of the objectively best consequences; and the kind that judges the rightness of an action in terms of the subjectively best consequences. For the Hitler case, we have already seen what conclusions would be judged "right" from the standpoint of (1) and (2), and how the choice dictated by (2) is preferable to that dictated by (1). But what about (3), and why does Russell prefer this approach over that of (2) as a basis for praise and blame? To answer this question, imagine a physician who is unaware of statistical evidence that a certain medication is slightly better for treating a circulatory problem than the one on which he has learned to rely. Imagine further that he regularly consults with his colleagues before prescribing medication to correct the circulatory ailment in question. Imagine that the reason he does so is to determine if there are better treatments available, and imagine that his colleagues are equally uninformed. Suppose further that our physician, who has not checked with his colleagues for a few weeks, is consulted by a patient with the circulatory problem in question. Our physician reflects on the fact that he has not consulted with his colleagues, but because of its effectiveness he prescribes the medication he is accustomed to prescribing for such cases. He has met Russell's condition by engaging in the "appropriate amount of candid thought." The particular circumstances of this case do not warrant his expending further time and effort regarding what course of action he should follow. We would never blame him for not doing so. This case validates Russell's claim that doing what is subjectively right can also be to do what is objectively wrong, and explains why Russell prefers (3) over (2) as a basis for praise and blame.

These contentions commit Russell to *act utilitarianism* as opposed to *rule utilitarianism*, a distinction which was not employed by philosophers at the time that Russell wrote the essay under consideration. Act utilitarianism adopts the utilitarian maxim, "always act to maximize the good in the world," and applies it directly to determine moral obligation. If telling a lie would, in certain circumstances, have better consequences than telling the truth, then one is obliged to lie in those circumstances. Rule utilitarianism, on the other hand, views the utilitarian maxim as the *underlying* justification for following certain rules. The rule utilitarian determines how he should act by consulting those rules which the maxim justifies. He would claim that the moral rule against lying is justified by the utilitarian maxim, that telling the truth will, in the long run, have better consequences than lying. No matter what are the particular circumstances surrounding his choice, he will abstain from lying, and tell the truth. Russell does, however, discuss moral codes, and recognizes both their importance for ethics, and the extent to which they are justified by consideration of consequences. He sounds like a rule utilitarian when he claims, regarding rules like those that comprise the Ten Commandments, that obedience to them "will in almost all cases have better consequences than disobedience; and the justification of the rules is not wholly independent of consequences."[9]   This recognition is, however, consistent with what I shall isolate, refer to as "subjective act consequentialism of the inclusive variety," and attribute to Russell.

Russell would not accept the classical formulation of the utilitarian maxim, "always act to maximize the good in the world." Since he claims that the agent has to be satisfied with intended or predictable consequences, and not actual ones, it follows that the agent can only be obliged to do what the agent judges will have the best consequences. Russell's view of this matter dictates the following reformulation of the utilitarian maxim, "act so as to maximize the *expectable* good in the world." We can mark the distinction between the kind of act utilitarianism which adopts the classic formulation of the utilitarian maxim, and the kind which adopts the reformulation dictated by Russell's views, as the distinction between *objective* and *subjective* act utilitarianism.

Subjective act utilitarianism has, however, been criticized for allowing the individual agent too much freedom of choice. Although an individual's acting in a specified way may well increase the happiness or good in the world, this same action would have disastrous consequences if everyone or even a majority did it. Whether or not, for example, a single individual pays her taxes will not appreciably add to or subtract from the good in the world. An individual who knows this might well choose not to pay his taxes because not doing so will have good consequences for his family. But if every taxpayer or even a majority of taxpayers reached the same kind of conclusion, and also refrained from paying their taxes, the consequences would be disastrous. Considerations of this sort can cause one to prefer rule consequentialism over act consequentialism because it recognizes the importance of our acting in concert in order to bring about optimal consequences. This criticism can be offset, however.

In the first place, rule utilitarianism is itself subject to serious objections. It implies that we are morally obliged to adhere to moral rules no matter what their consequences might be. It would dictate unacceptable choices. It would, for example, prohibit lying in order to save lives. Besides, act utilitarianism does not preclude following rules. To claim that we should always act to bring about the best results is compatible with the idea that we must sometimes follow rules, and this emendation is, as I pointed out previously, consistent with what Russell says about rule following.

This emendation, or *inclusive formulation* of act utilitarianism, will not resolve the problem exemplified by the taxes case, however. Since any one of us can imagine some use for our tax money which would produce greater happiness than would accrue from its use by the government, any one of us, acting on our own, will be forced to ignore the rule and make an exception of ourselves. The disastrous consequences that would accrue if most or even many of us actually refused to pay our taxes will not be a relevant consideration in the individual's assessment of his specific action. It would seem that the advantages that are amassed by rule-following behavior cannot exist unless the majority engages in the relevant practices, and this can best be accomplished by a rule form of consequentialism which considers the rules to be *prima facie* rules--rules that determine what we should do unless there are overriding considerations to the contrary. And, although this might seem to imply that Russell would have been proven wiser had he adopted a *prima facie* version of rule utilitarianism rather than an act version of it, appearances can be deceptive.

The *prima facie* version dictates that the agent will always have to evaluate the particular circumstances surrounding his intended action to determine whether it is a case where moral rules should be followed, or one where overriding conditions render them inapplicable. The agent never bases his moral decisions upon the rules themselves. Instead, he always has to decide whether or not to act in accordance with a rule. The upshot of this consideration is that the situationistic form of rule utilitarianism cannot be distinguished from what I previously referred to as inclusive act utilitarianism.

Moreover, we can offset the kind of objection which Russell's form of act utilitarianism encounters when faced with the taxes kind of case if we utilize Parfit's (1984) terminology, and distinguish between an *individualistic* and a *collective* interpretation of inclusive act utilitarianism. A collective interpretation of inclusive act utilitarianism would interpret the utilitarian maxim to require always acting in those ways, and sometimes this would amount to following rules, which would, if we acted collectively or as a group, maximize the good in the world. This interpretation would impose upon the agent an obligation to pay his taxes. Nothing which Russell says would preclude interpreting his views as favoring the collective interpretation of inclusive subjective act utilitarianism. Support for this interpretation is evidenced by his having claimed, as I pointed out previously, that adherence to rules like those that constitute the Ten Commandments "will in almost all cases have better consequences than disobedience."

Aside from the difficulties inherent in Russell's idea that goodness is a quality, and that rational intuition or conscience must be combined with consequentialism in order to gain a complete account of right and wrong--ideas he abandons in *Human Society in Ethics and Politics*--the ethical theory which he espouses in "The Elements of Ethics" is largely defensible. I have already offered what amounts to a defense of those aspects of his theory consistent with what I have referred to as the collective interpretation of inclusive act utilitarianism.

At the beginning of this chapter, I claimed that Russell is right and Ayer is wrong as regards whether or not ethics should be treated as part of, rather than in contrast to, science. It seems clear to me that moral rules are founded upon or originate in a set of complex practices employed by human beings to promote harmonious coexistence between themselves and, as a result, to diminish fear, pain, and suffering. We are disposed to act, and to determine how we ought to act, in a fashion which is consequentialistic in nature. This underlying consequentialist-based set of moral *practices* is both the *impetus* of and the *basis* for whatever credibility any form of consequentialism possesses. Most importantly, however, these ethical practices are, when properly understood and freed from religious creeds and philosophical obscurity, as determinate and justified as any other empirical phenomena-- they are *confirmable* through experience.

When I talk about confirmation in ethics I am simply talking about moral rules being accepted or rejected on the basis of observable results. A moral rule at its inception is little more than an unconfirmed but plausible "hypothesis." In science when we formulate an hypothesis, we are venturing an explanation for certain observed phenomenon, and having done so, we engage in the construction of experimental contexts which will confirm or disconfirm our hypothesis. Ethics did not develop in parallel fashion. Still, it does make sense to talk about the empirical consequences of behavior in accordance with a rule or practice. And what is more, one can talk meaningfully about human history as the experimental context which serves to confirm or disconfirm the effectiveness of various practices, including ethical ones. Take, for example, the widespread practice of building roads and maintaining them. Clearly this practice can be justified by its consequences even though it did not originate in strict scientific fashion. Historically, human trails came to be, the way deer trails come to be, a means of getting as efficiently as possible to a source of basic need satisfaction, for example, palatable drinking water. In time, as humans became more and more cognitively efficient, they came to recognize the advantage of such trails, and hence to construct even better trails, and to maintain them, and this eventually led to the complex and highly efficient highway systems of today. By instinct we know that certain actions are necessary for our survival. It is not by instinct that we know that well developed and maintained roadways provide distinct advantages over those that are not well planned or maintained. This is something we had to learn. It has been confirmed by our experiences.

The science of ethics, like any scientific enterprise, is a dynamic and flexible activity, subject to modification on the basis of new and unexpected discoveries. Innovations in science and technology create new problems for ethics. Cloning, *in vitro* fertilization, organ transplants, the computer internet, etc., force us to rethink our moral practices, and adjust them to cover such innovations. When we do so, what we do is venture an hypothesis as regards the outcome of modifying our practices to adjudicate emergent realities. Whether or not such an hypothesis will survive the test of time is always an open question.

I have been defending the *substance* of Russell's empirical approach to ethics. I disagree with him regarding the its *details*. I will postpone discussion of these details until after I have examined his later work, *Human Society in Ethics and Politics*. Only in this later work does Russell express his ethical theory in sufficient detail for its flaws to become evident.

In *Human Society in Ethics and Politics*, Russell retains his commitment to consequentialism, in so far as he retains the idea that the rightness of an action can be determined by probable consequences, but abandons his commitment to intuitionism. He also, somewhat reluctantly, gives up the idea that goodness is an non-natural property. Here, he acknowledges just how much disagreement exists between cultures, nations, religions, and even individuals as regards what we ought to do, a fact which he explicates in detail.[10] From his observations about the widespread disagreements about moral codes or what we ought and ought not to do, he concludes that our only hope for some kind of objectivity in ethics is to discover some end "which conduct should serve, and to judge conduct to be "right" when it is calculated to promote this end." This leads him to further conclude that "good" and "bad," rather than "right" and "wrong" are "the fundamental concepts of ethics."[11] He then explicates the concept of "good" as *intrinsic* good, in contrast to *instrumental* good. He says, "A thing is 'good,' as I wish to use the term, if it is valued for its own sake and not only for its effects."[12] He then proceeds by defining "good" as "satisfaction of desire,"[13] and then to distinguish between "partial" and "general" goods. He defines the latter as "the total satisfaction of desire, no matter by whom enjoyed." Partial goods are those goods which give satisfaction to some individuals or groups while denying satisfaction to other individuals or groups.

An ambiguity manifests itself here, however. By the "general good," one could mean either what would give satisfaction to all or most members of society, or the sum total of satisfaction occurring in the world at a given time, minus the dissatisfaction also present at that time. One could argue that pleasure, or some other intrinsic value, is the general good. But one could also argue that the total amount of pleasure, minus the pain, in the world at a given period in history is the general good. Any theory assuming the latter idea of the general good is encumbered by the classic objection to consequentialism.

Satisfying the interests of a majority of a given population while at the same time thwarting the interests of the minority segment of that same population can maximize the general good, and do so even though the minority group may have to suffer great cruelties. Slavery provides a compelling example of this kind of inequity. It benefits the ruling majority, but creates unbelievable hardships and pain for the slaves. Where it exists, its abolition is the only equitable solution. This is unfortunate for the theory in question, however. Because of the unhappy consequences that would result for the ruling majority, the abolishment of slavery would appear to create considerably more unhappiness in the world than its retention. For this reason, the theory in question would be forced to adopt an *inequitable* course of action. It would be compelled to advocate the retention of slavery.

If, however, one conceives of the general good in the first sense I previously introduced, namely as, "what would give satisfaction to all or most members of society," one can answer this kind of objection. Russell does, recognize the importance of the general good over that of the individual. He says that the, "main purpose of morality is to promote behavior serving the interests of the group, and not merely the individual." But our ability to accomplish this end depends upon our ability to answer the question, "What would maximize satisfaction for most or all members of society?" One can answer this question in a satisfactorily by claiming that it is "harmonious coexistence." Moral rules are simply empirically (as opposed to logically) necessary conditions for the promotion of harmonious co-existence among humans. Transgression of the equal rights principle by the majority creates an intolerable kind of existence for those members of society who are disenfranchised by such infraction, and eventually leads to civil unrest, riots, and revolution. So although satisfying the majority of the populace by frustrating the minority segment of that same populace will, in a given *time slice*, maximize the good, it will eventually bring about much suffering and pain for all concerned, and render harmonious coexistence impossible.

Russell does not recognize the ambiguity I have been at pain to explicate, but he does wrestle with the kind of difficulties the latter concept of the general good generates, including the slavery issue. He attempts to resolve controversies such as the kind generated by the demands of conflicting groups--slave owners versus slaves, one nation, religion, family, etc. versus another--by reducing such controversies to the conflicting demands of conscience. Theoretical resolution of such conflicts can, according to Russell, best be accomplished by the development of an "objective" test of rightness of conscience.[14]

As far as Russell is concerned, the central question in ethics is "is there anything in ethics that is not, in the last analysis, subjective?" He claims that it can best be answered if we first establish "a series of fundamental propositions and definitions" which comprise "a body of coherent ethical propositions," and which are "true (or false) in the same sense as if they were propositions of science."[15] The set which he arrives at can be simplified and stated as follows:

(1) Those acts which are approved of are those believed likely to have, on balance, effects of certain kinds, and those which are disapproved of are those likely to have the opposite effects,

(2) approved of actions are defined as "good," and disapproved of actions as "bad,"

(3) "right actions" are defined as those actions which, on the available evidence, will most likely have the best consequences of those which are possible, these other possibilities he defines as "wrong,"

(4) it is right to approve of right actions and to disapprove of those which are wrong.

Although Russell's claims that this set of basic ethical principles are true or false in the same sense as are the propositions of science, he insists that they are descriptive of "emotion and feeling, the emotion of approval and the feeling of enjoyment and satisfaction." It is the emotion of approval which, according to Russell, is "involved in the definition" of "right" and "wrong," and it is the feeling of enjoyment and satisfaction which "is involved in the definition" of "intrinsic value."[16] It is in the light of these contentions that I can clarify my earlier claim that while I agree with Russell regarding the descriptive nature of ethics, I disagree with him as regards the details. As I pointed out above, my view is that moral rules, for example, "One ought not lie," are themselves confirmable, that they are simply abbreviations of complex practices which have been confirmed to produce widespread happiness by making it possible for us to live together harmoniously. I would agree that the claims which Russell alleges regarding our emotions and feelings are true, but I would hasten to point out that an ethics based upon these facts lacks objective justification. In both of Russell's works on ethics he stresses the importance of consequences for an objective account of ethics. He acknowledges that the main purpose of morality is to promote behavior serving the interests of the group, and not merely the individual. But he fails to take the crucial step and delineate ethics as a set of principles or practices which can be confirmed to have accomplished the interest of the group. His account of ethics is inherently a causal account. He finds the causes for the existence of ethics in human emotions and feelings. He fails, however, to grasp the distinction between an *explanation* of ethics, and a *justification* of it. Both can be accomplished empirically. He confuses the two, and while he offers an empirical or causal account of ethics, he fails to fully appreciate, because of his confusion, that consequentialism is itself not only the basis for objectivity in ethics, it is also its justification.

Endnotes

1 Nowell-Smith (1954).

2 Russell, (1910) p. 13.

3 Ayer (1972) pp. 129-130.

4 Russell (1910) p. 15.

5 Ibid., p. 21.

6 Ibid., p. 21.

7 Ibid., pp. 30- 31.

8 Ibid., pp. 32-36.

9 Ibid., p. 29.

10 Russell, (1955) pp. 17- 30.

11 Ibid., p. 26.

12 Ibid., p. 31.

13 Ibid., p. 36.

14 Ibid., p. 61.

15 Ibid., p. 91.

16 Ibid., pp. 92-98.

17 Ibid., p. 100.

VII

God, Religion and the Meaning of Life

Like most people, Russell was raised to believe in God. Like most Englishmen, he was taught both at home and at school to be a Christian. But, like most people of philosophical and intellectual ability, he inevitably began to have doubts about both God's existence and about the Christian faith. Eventually, he became both an agnostic and an anti-Christian.

In his early teens, inspired in part by his grandmother's influence, Russell claims that he became "passionately interested in religion, and set to work to examine successively the arguments for free will, immortality, and God." He discarded belief in both free will and immortality before doing so for belief in God. He continued to believe in God until he was eighteen because he believed that the first cause proof for God's existence had to be valid. But at eighteen, influenced by reading John Stuart Mill's autobiography, he realized that the first cause argument was fallacious, and became an agnostic. Throughout his life he continued to be an agnostic, and an opponent of the Christian religion as well as religion in general.

He entered Cambridge at about the same time that he gave up belief in God's existence, and through the influence of his teachers, some of the most influential of whom were Platonists and Hegelians, he sought religious satisfaction in philosophy. Even after he abandoned Hegel, he continued to admire the eternal and timeless world conceived of by Plato. In his twenties he began to take seriously the work of Spinoza. Spinoza's pantheistic religion had great appeal to Russell at this time and it continued for many years to influence his views about the meaning of life. He was always aware, however, that the passion which mysticism aroused in him, like the hotness of blood characteristic of Thoroughbred horses, had to be held in check by the bridle of logic and science. Unbridled enthusiasm, like an unbridled Thoroughbred, is apt to take one places best left untraveled.

Throughout his life, Russell argued against the various versions of the classical "proofs" for God's existence, namely, the ontological, the cosmological, and the teleological proofs. He encapsulated his assessment of these proofs for God's existence by saying that only someone already convinced that God existed would find them at all convincing. He claimed that people are led to believe in God's existence not by intellectual proofs, but by education. They are taught to believe in God's existence, and that is the principle reason they do so. But he also adds that such beliefs are based on emotional, not rational, grounds.[1]

An *explanation* for why people believe in God's existence is one thing, a *justification* for this belief is another. The desire to believe in God has many explanations, but according to Russell, it is primarily motivated by feelings of fear. Justification of this belief cannot be accomplished by deductive means, according to Russell, because it is an empirical matter. Russell's position on this matter is best represented by an often repeated antidote. Supposedly, at ninety, while attending a dinner party, he was asked by a woman who was offended by his agnosticism what he would say if, after he died, he was confronted by God. His answer is reputed to have been, "Why did you provide so little evidence of your own existence?"

Throughout most of his life, Russell was an opponent of Christianity. He argued not only that its major figure Jesus Christ may not have actually existed, but that even if he did, he certainly was neither "superlatively wise" nor "superlatively good." He claimed that Socrates was more worthy of veneration than Christ.[2]

Against the view that Christ was superlatively wise, Russell cites as evidence Gospel narratives. He points out that Christ told his followers such things as: "Ye shall not have gone over the cities of Israel till the Son of Man be come;" "There are some standing here which shall not taste death till the Son of Man come into his kingdom;" and "Take no thought of tomorrow." Russell interprets these quotations to be evidence that Christ believed that his second coming would take place during the lifetime of many of those who were present when he said these things. Russell points out that his followers did believe that he would return soon, and they acted accordingly. They neglected their everyday concerns, and of course were disappointed. Since these people did believe that his second coming was imminent, Christ cannot have been very wise, and certainly not superlatively so. As evidence against the Christian dogma that Christ was superlatively good, Russell also cites the Gospels. He was offended by the fact that Christ was willing to condemn non-believers to the eternal flames of hell. He was particularly offended by Christ saying, "Ye serpents, ye generation of vipers, how can ye escape the damnation of Hell," and "Whosoever speaketh against the Holy Ghost it shall not be forgiven him neither in this world or the world to come." He even speculates that Christ must have taken a certain satisfaction out of the fact that sinners and non-believers would suffer "wailing and the gnashing of teeth," because He talks about their wailing and gnashing of teeth so often. Russell finds it hard to believe that even a moderately good person, much less One who is superlatively good, would instill in other human beings such "fears and terrors."[3]

Russell also argued against Christianity because it has very often retarded progress both in science and in society, and because it is directly responsible for much human pain and suffering. According to Russell, "every single bit of progress in humane feeling" has been opposed by the Christian Church, and that it "still is the principle enemy of moral progress in the world." And, moreover, that science has had to force its way "step by step against the Christian Religion" for its very existence.[4] As examples of the pain and suffering which Christianity has perpetuated, Russell cites such things as the Crusades and the burning of witches. He was particularly horrified by the fact that, as a result of the biblical exhortation, "Thou shalt not suffer a witch to live," more than one hundred thousand woman were put to death in Germany alone between 1450 and 1550.[5]

For these reasons, as well as others too numerous to consider in the present work, Russell abandoned his belief in the God of Christianity. He did not, however, abandon what may well be the essence of religion, namely, the need to find some kind of meaning in life. In 1901, while he and his first wife Alys were sharing a house with his friend and collaborator Alfred North Whitehead, and his wife Evelyn, Russell had a mystical experience which he claimed transformed his life. He referred to it as a "conversion." Evelyn, for whom he felt a great deal of affection, was at the time suffering from a serious heart condition. One evening, Russell and Alys returned home from having attended a reading by Gilbert Murray of part of his translation of The Hippolytus to find Evelyn in great pain, pain so great that she appeared to be completely cut off from everyone. Russell claims to have been profoundly affected by her sense of "solitude." He perceived it to be the very essence of human existence.[6]

Many years later, Russell attempted to characterize the mystical experience. He described it as fourfold in character involving: (1) the intuitive grasp of reality; (2) belief in a reality which is unified; (3) belief that time is unreal; and (4) the belief that evil is also unreal. And although at this later date, guided by analysis and reason, he concludes that the mystical creed as encapsulated in these four characteristics is mistaken, he remains convinced that "there is an element of wisdom to be learned from the mystical way of feeling." This feeling or emotion, although responsible for the mistaken creed of the mystic, is, nonetheless, he claims, "the inspirer of whatever is best in Man." Even science, which seems antithetical to mysticism, can, he says, be "fostered and nourished by that very spirit of reverence in which mysticism lives and moves."[7]

While recognizing the significance of the mystical experience, Russell wisely restrained from drawing the kinds of inferences that many are led to draw from it. He did not reject the world, abandon his profession, book passage to Nepal, don a saffron robe, and seek fulfillment at the knee of some holy man.   Instead he retained his objectivity, and remained true to his inherently skeptical nature. In fact, in the same work from which I just quoted, Russell expresses, in the section entitled "A Free Man's Worship," an extremely pessimistic and nihilistic view of human existence. The views he expresses in this work are remarkably similar to those expressed by the existentialists, specifically, Sartre and Camus. He shares Sartre's concerns regarding mankind's place in nature, given that belief in God's existence is no longer a rational alternative. Like Camus, he advocates a kind of heroic defiance of the fates as the only way to cope with the pessimism and nihilism created by skepticism about God's existence. For without God the universe appears to be purposeless, indifferent, unfriendly, filled with unpleasantness, and ultimately fatal. He concludes this essay with the following paragraph:

> Brief and Powerless is man's life: on him and all his race the slow, sure doom falls pitiless and dark. Blind to good and evil, reckless of destruction, omnipotent matter rolls on its relentless way; for Man, condemned to-day to lose his dearest to-morrow himself to pass through the gate of darkness, it remains only to cherish, ere yet the blow falls, the lofty thoughts that ennoble his little day: disdaining the coward terrors of the slave of Fate, to worship at the shrines that his own hands have built: undismayed by the empire of chance, to preserve a mind free from the wanton tyranny that rules his outward life; proudly, defiant of the irresistible forces that tolerate, for a moment, his knowledge and his condemnation, to sustain alone, a weary but unyielding Atlas, the world that his own ideals have fashioned despite the trampling march of unconscious power.[8]

Although this pessimistic and nihilistic view of man's place in nature is in stark contrast to the more optimistic view he sometimes adopted, and although it was written at a time of crisis in Russell's life, it is representative of that omnipresent tendency of Russell's toward skepticism. Nihilism as regards the meaning of life is in part the consequence of epistemological skepticism. Thomas Nagel, one of, if not the most influential of contemporary philosophers concerned with the meaning of life issue, incorporates epistemological skepticism as a necessary condition in his argument in favor of the idea that life is absurd.[9]

I find it surprising that some commentators on Russell's philosophy want to make some kind of religious believer out of him. Some have gone so far as to claim that while his philosophical view, based on reason, was that of an agnostic, his behavior and comments to friends, particularly, one might note with a tidbit of sarcasm, to his love interests, are at odds with his philosophy. They argue that his behavior and life are those of a man who fervently believes in God.[10] This view has nothing to recommend it. It is little more than a desire on the part of those who are convinced of God's existence to find an ally in the person of someone so obviously brilliant, and influential as

Russell!

It is best to let Russell speak on his own behalf. Summarizing a lifetime of concern regarding the meaning of human existence, he said, at the age of seventy one:

> I have always ardently desired to find some justification for the emotions inspired by certain things that seem to stand outside human life and to deserve feelings of awe...Those who attempt to make a religion of humanism, which recognizes nothing greater than man, do not satisfy my emotions. And yet I am unable to believe that, in the world as known, there is anything that I can value outside human beings, and, to a much lesser extent, animals. Not the starry heavens, but their effects upon human percipients, have excellence; to admire the universe for its size is slavish and absurd; And so my intellect goes with the humanists, though my emotions violently rebel. In this respect the "consolations of philosophy" are not for me. In more purely intellectual ways, on the contrary I have found as much satisfaction in philosophy as any one could reasonably have expected.[11]

Endnotes

[1] Seckel (1986) p. 65-69.

[2] Ibid., p. 67.

[3] Ibid., pp. 66-69.

[4] Ibid., pp. 69-71.

[5] Russell (1955) p. 11.

[6] Russell (1951) p. 193.

[7] Russell (1927) pp. 25-29.

[8] Russell (1927) p. 14.

[9] Nagel (1971).

[10] Brightman (1944).

[11] Russell (1943) p. 19.

BIBLIOGRAPHY

Austin, J. L. (1962) *How to do Things with Words*, (Cambridge
    Massachusetts: Harvard University Press).
Ayer, A. J. (1936) *Language Truth and Logic*, 2nd edition (New York:
    Dover Publications, Inc.).
    (1972) *Bertrand Russell, Modern Masters*, ed. Frank Kermode
    (New York: The Viking Press).
C. P. Baker and P.M.S. Hacker (1984) *Language, Sense & Nonsense*
    (Oxford: Basil Blackwell).
Brightman, Edgar S. (1944) "Russell's Philosophy of Religion" in
    Schlipp (1944) Vol. II, pp. 539-556.
Carnap, Rudolph (1932) "The Elimination of Metaphysics Through
    Logical Analysis of Language" reprinted in *Logical
    Positivism*, ed. A. J. Ayer (New York: The Free Press, 1959).
Churchland, Paul (1984) *Matter and Consciousness* (Cambridge, Mass.:
    Harvard University Press).
Godel, Kurt (1944) "Russell's Mathematical Logic" in Schlipp (1944)
Grice H. P. (1967) "Logic and Conversation," reprinted in *The Logic
    of Grammar*, ed. Donald Davidson and Gilbert Harman (Encino
    and Belmont, California: Dickenson Publishing Company,
    Inc., 1975) pp. 64-75.
Hacker, P.M.S. (1996) *Wittgenstein's Place in Twentieth Century
    Analytic Philosophy* (Oxford: Blackwell Publishers).
Kneale, William and Martha (1962) *The Development of Logic*
    (Oxford: The Clarendon Press).
Kolak, Daniel (1998) *Wittgenstein's Tractatus* (Mountain View
    California: Mayfield Publishing Company).

Linsky, Leonard (1967) *Referring* (New York: Humanities Press).

Moore, G. E. (1959) "Four Forms of Skepticism" originally published in *Philosophical Papers* (London: George Allen & Unwin LTD).

(1936) "Is Existence a Predicate?" reprinted in *Philosophical Papers* (London: George Allen & Unwin LTD, 1959).

(1952) *The Philosophy of G. E. Moore*, The Library of Living Philosophers, ed. Paul Arthur Schlipp (New York: Tudor Publishing Company).

Nagel, Thomas (1971) "The Absurd," *The Journal of Philosophy*, pp. 716-727.

Nowell-Smith, P.H. (1954) *Ethics* (Harmondsworth, Middlesex: Penguin Books).

Odell, S. Jack (1984) "A Paraphrastic Theory of Meaning," *Theoretical Linguistics*, Vol. 11, No. 3.

Odell, S. Jack and James F. Zartman (1982) "A Defensible Formulation of the Verification Principle," *Metaphilosophy*, Vol. 13, 1.

Parfit, Derek (1984) *Reasons and Persons* (New York: Oxford University Press).

Reichenbach, Hans (1944) "Bertrand Russell's Logic" Schlipp (1944).

Russell, B. (1903) *The Principles of Mathematics* (London: Allen & Unwin).

(1905) "On Denoting" Davidson and Harman (1975).

(1908) "Mathematical Logic as Based on the Theory of Type" American Journal of Mathematics, XXX, pp. 222-262, reprinted in *Logic and Knowledge*, pp. 59-102.

(1910) *Principia Mathematica to *56* (Cambridge, England: Cambridge University Press, 1964).

(1910) "The Elements of Ethics" in *Philosophical Essays* Revised Edition (1966) (London: Allen & Unwin LTD).

(1912) *The Problems of Philosophy* (New York: A Galaxy Book, Oxford University Press, 1959).

(1917) "A Free Man's Worship" from *Mysticism and Logic* (London: Allen & Unwin).

(1918) "The Philosophy of Logical Atomism" reprinted in *Logic and Knowledge*, ed. by Robert C. Marsh (London: George Allen & Unwin, 1956).

(1927) *Selected Papers of Bertrand Russell* (New York: Random House, The Modern Library).

(1929) *Our Knowledge of the External World*, 2nd Edition

(New York: Mentor Book, The New American Library, 1960)
Delivered as Lowell Lectures in 1914.

(1940) *An Inquiry into Meaning and Truth* (Baltimore,
Maryland: Pelican Book, 1961).

(1943) "My Mental Development" in Schilpp (1944).

(1945) *The History of Western Philosophy: Its connection
with Political and Social circumstances from the Earliest
Times to the Present Day* (New York: Simon and Schuster).

(1946) "Mind and Matter in Modern Science" reprinted in
Bertrand Russell On God and Religion, ed. by Al Seckel
(Buffalo, New York: Prometheus Books, 1986) pp. 151-163.

(1948) *Human Knowledge: Its Scope and Limits* (New York:
Simon and Schuster, 1964).

(1948) "A Broadcast Debate on BBC Between Russell and
Father F. C. Copleston, S. J." reproduced in *Classical and
Contemporary Readings in the Philosophy of Religion*, ed.
John Hicks (Englewood Cliffs, N. J.: Prentice-Hall, 1964).

(1951) *The Autobiography of Bertrand Russell: The Middle
Years: 1914-1944* (New York: Bantam Book Edition, 1967).

(1951) *The Autobiography of Bertrand Russell: The Early
Years: 1872-World War I* (New York: Bantam Book Edition,
1967).

(1955) *Human Society in Ethics and Politics*, (New York:
Simon and Schuster).

(1972) *My Own Philosophy* (Hamilton, Ontario: McMaster
University Library Press).

Schlipp, P. A. (1944) *The Philosophy of Bertrand Russell* New York:
Harper Torchbooks, The Academy Library, Harper & Row).

Strawson, P. F. (1950) "On Referring" reprinted in *Philosophy and
Ordinary Language*, ed. Charles E. Caton (Urbana, Illinois:
The University of Illinois Press, 1963).

(1952) *Introduction to Logical Theory* (London: Methuen &
Co.).

Urmson, J. O. (1956) *Philosophical Analysis: It's Development
Between the Two Wars* (Oxford: The Clarendon Press).

Wittgenstein, L. (1922) *Tractatus Logico Philosophicus* (London:
Routledge & Kegan Paul. LTD.).

(1958) *Philosophical Investigations* (New York: Macmillan
Publishing Co., Inc.).